WILDCATS
IN THE
HOUSE

BOOKS BY STEVE RUSSO

Fabulous Funny Jokes for Kids

Jammin' Jokes for Kids

Fear No Evil?

They All Can't Be Right: Do All Spiritual Paths Lead to God?

What's the Deal With Wicca?

SPIRITUAL STUFF YOU CAN GET
FROM HIGH SCHOOL MUSICAL

WILDCATS
IN THE
HOUSE

STEVE RUSSO AND GABI RUSSO

BETHANYHOUSE
PUBLISHERS

Published by Bethany House Publishers
11400 Hampshire Avenue South
Bloomington, Minnesota 55438

Bethany House Publishers is a division of
Baker Publishing Group, Grand Rapids, Michigan.

Printed in the United States of America

Library of Congress Cataloging-in-Publication Data

Russo, Steve, 1953-
    Wildcats in the house : spiritual stuff you can get from High school musical / Steve Russo and Gabi Russo.
        p. cm.
    Summary: "Examines the Disney Channel's popular 'High School Musical' and offers guidance in finding the biblical principles represented in the TV movie's songs, characters, and storyline"—Provided by publisher.
    ISBN-13: 978-0-7642-0456-2 (pbk.)
    ISBN-10: 0-7642-0456-4 (pbk.)
    1. High school musical (Motion picture) 2. Motion pictures—Moral and ethical aspects. I. Russo, Gabi. II. Title.
    PN1997.2.H54R87 2007
    791.43'72—dc22   2007015018

For the "Wildcats" in my house: Tony, Kati, and Gabi.

You rock my world and make life fun!

ABOUT THE AUTHORS

Steve Russo is an internationally known communicator and the author of fourteen books. He is a television personality, host of the daily radio feature *Real Answers,* and was co-host of Focus on the Family's weekly teen talk radio show *Life on the Edge—Live!* Steve is a professional drummer and a member of the Recording Academy. He makes his home in Southern California.

Gabi Russo is Steve's eleven-year-old daughter. Her favorite subjects in school are math and history, and she's active in sports (swimming and soccer) and music (clarinet). She enjoys traveling, reading, hanging out with friends, bugging her brother and sister, and especially wearing out her *High School Musical* CD and DVD.

CONTENTS

INTRODUCTION

Everyone's talking about *High School Musical*. It's huge!

Who do you relate to most in the movie? Troy the basketball boy; Gabriella the freaky math girl; Ice Princess Sharpay; ditzy Ryan; Troy's best friend, Chad; or maybe Taylor, the leader of East High's scholastic decathlon team? It's easy to find someone you can connect with in this fun and zany movie.

Has it given you earworms yet? I'm not talking about the slimy creatures that crawl around in your backyard. Earworms are words, pictures, and lyrics you can't get out of your mind—no matter how hard you try! You get earworms from the things you read, watch, and listen to.

Here's what I mean: I bet I can give you titles of some of the tunes that Troy, Gabriella, Sharpay, and Ryan sing, and you'll immediately know all the words. Let's try it with just a few songs from the movie:

"Start of Something New"

"Stick to the Status Quo"

"Get'cha Head in the Game"

"We're All in This Together"

Okay, you can stop singing and dancing for a minute. Do you see what I mean? Amazing—you probably didn't even need to see the karaoke version of the movie to sing all the words!

But now that you have the words—and the cool dances that go with each tune—in your head, maybe there's something more we can learn from the East High Wildcats about ourselves and others.

As Troy, Gabriella, and the rest of the Wildcats reach for the stars and follow their dreams—singing and dancing—we can learn about things like peer pressure, being yourself, loneliness, acceptance, and teamwork. Along the way we're going to check out some wise advice from a book that's been read by more people than any other book in history. And we're going to have fun doing it!

Talk about fun. I had a blast working on this book with my daughter, Gabi. She's the one who first introduced me to *High School Musical*. Besides attending middle school, playing clarinet, and hanging with friends, Gabi loves to do anything that has to do with *High School Musical*.

After about the fifth time I watched the movie with her, and after listening to the CD soundtrack nearly every day for several weeks, I got the idea to write a book about all the spiritual stuff you can get from the movie. So I started asking Gabi questions about the characters and songs from the movie. She was amazing! Gabi knew all the scenes plus the lyrics for every song. Sometimes she'd even act out different parts of the movie—she gets crazy sometimes! The next thing I knew, she and I were working on *Wildcats in the House* together. Hey, maybe this is the start of something new—a writing team! Look out, 'cause who knows what Steve and Gabi will come up with next! In the meantime, let's see what kind of stuff we can learn from the gang at East High.

So let's get ready to "rock the house"!

1

TAKE A CHANCE

Troy and Gabriella meet by chance at a New Year's Eve party while on vacation. Neither one really wants to be at the party, but they both get chosen for karaoke and end up rockin' the house with their song "Start of Something New."

After they finish singing, Troy and Gabriella introduce themselves to each other. Tonight has been something new for each of them. Troy's usual microphone is the showerhead because basketball is his life, while Gabriella's only previous singing experience was in the church choir. Her comfort zone is being curled up in a chair reading a book. But they both say how much they liked their New Year's Eve performance.

Gabi says:
Even though you might be afraid, you should always try something new. Good things just might happen to you.

The party is interrupted by fireworks as the New Year is ushered in. Just before they say good-bye, Troy and Gabriella exchange cell numbers and pictures—promising to call one another later.

Gabi says:
I love the karaoke scene in the movie. I think it would be a cool part to be in because Troy and Gabriella looked like they were having fun.

At the party Troy and Gabriella took a big risk—even though they were forced into it. Remember the emcee who leaned over to them on stage and said, "Someday you'll thank me for this"? At first they were both nervous and uncomfortable, but by the end of the song they were having fun singing and dancing on stage.

Have you ever been in a situation like Troy's and Gabriella's, where you felt like you were being forced to try something new? I mean something more than eating a strange-looking vegetable at your aunt's house during a family gathering. I've had lots of experiences like this—including one that happened the first week of eighth grade at Hopkins Junior High. But before I tell you what happened, you need to know something about me when I was a teenager.

WET SOCKS

When I was a teen, especially in junior high, I didn't like myself and had a terrible self-image. Besides being tall and skinny, I had dark curly hair (which I totally hated), two fangs sticking out of the front of my mouth, and a huge honkin' nose. I was totally self-conscious, and I guess that's why I hid behind my drums—because that was the only place I really felt comfortable. I thought I could get people to like me as "the drummer dude."

During the summer between seventh and eighth grade, showers were installed in our gym locker rooms. My friends and I weren't all that excited about the news when we heard, but I guess the teachers thought showers would help with the "air pollution" in the classrooms. The big day finally came during the first week of school when my buddies and I would have to take our first public shower. Yikes! I could hardly sleep the night before. Mom couldn't figure out why I hardly touched my breakfast, but my stomach was in knots. I was worried about what my buddies would say once they saw me without my baggy clothes on.

Everything went fine during gym class. We were used to changing into our gym shorts and shirts. And most of us just wore the same shoes and socks all day long—it was too much of a hassle to bring extras to school. Plus, none of us changed our underwear for gym class. Talk about "air pollution"—gross! But today would be different. Coach said that from now on, we had to take showers at the end of class. He even said we had to use soap!

Gabi says:
Ew! 'Bout time you used soap!

We kept stalling when it was time to hit the showers. "Couldn't we just shoot a few more hoops?" we asked our coach. He finally blew his whistle and said, "Gentlemen, put the balls in the equipment room on your way in and hit the showers." Now it was my turn to stall some more. I was the last one standing at my locker. I was trying to figure a way out of this new experience. I heard the showers click on and my buddies say, "Come on in, Russo—you big wimp. This isn't so bad." I couldn't keep stalling any longer. So I shut my locker and headed toward the showers.

I turned the water on and stepped in. *Hey, this isn't so bad after all,* I thought. I started to soap up. Then it happened. At first it was over on my right side. Then I heard it on my left. Pretty soon the entire shower room erupted into laughter as I heard my buddies say, "Hey, look at Russo—he's taking a shower with his socks on!" I had been so afraid that someone was going to laugh at me that I forgot to take off my socks! Not only did my buddies tease me the rest of the day, but I had to wear wet socks because I hadn't brought another pair to school with me. My new experience in taking showers at school didn't start off very well. And it's definitely gotta be one of my most embarrassing moments!

Gabi says:
That's hilarious!

RISK-TAKER

You've probably never had a shower experience like that. But even when you don't feel like you're being forced to do something new, stepping out of your comfort zone can be risky. Maybe for you it was learning to ride a skateboard or learning to swim. How many times did you fall off your board before you started having fun riding down the street? Or how much water did you swallow before you felt comfortable swimming in a pool or a lake?

Just like Troy and Gabriella experienced doing something new like karaoke at the party, most of the time, once you get the hang of the "new thing" you've tried—you like it! But some new things can be more risky than others—especially when it comes to hangin' with friends and being in relationships.

No one wants to fail in that area of life. Let's face it—we all want to fit in and be accepted. No one wants to be rejected and hurt. But unfortunately, relationships can be risky business. And if we don't figure out how to develop healthy friendships early, it only gets worse as we get older. There are lots of other areas in life that also require us to be risk-takers.

A risk-taker is a person who's not afraid of failure. They're willing to take chances in order to learn new things. Sometimes being a risk-taker can be dangerous—depending on what new thing you're trying to do.

Now, before you run off and decide to try cliff-diving without anyone watching out for you, or riding your skateboard on the center divider of the closest major highway, STOP and THINK. Consider the consequences of the risk you're about to take. Imagine there's a yellow caution light in the front of your brain—just like the ones you see on stoplights. When drivers see the yellow light, they know it's a warning that the light is about to turn red, and they need to be careful and slow down. Let this imaginary yellow caution light in the front of your mind remind you to slow down and think before you act. Before you decide to try something new—take a risk—ask yourself, *If I do this, is there a danger to me physically? To someone else? Will taking this risk have a long-term effect on my life? Is now the right time for me to try something new? Would my parents approve of what I'm about to do?*

Being a risk-taker doesn't mean you have to put yourself in a dangerous or negative situation. But most risk-taking can be positive because it's helpful in discovering your true identity—who you really are. Trying new things can open up all kinds of fun experiences in your life. There's always the risk of failure or, at the very least, finding out you don't like something. But it's worth the risk. Just think about what you might be missing if you don't try something new.

Take food, for example. I've traveled to a lot of countries around the world. I've tasted some amazing food and some food that was pretty disgusting, too. But I made up my mind a long time ago that I will try something at least once—that is, as long as it doesn't smell really disgusting or look totally bizarre. I'm glad I made this decision because I would have missed out on tasting some incredible food!

Gabi says:
If you really want to try something new or different, you should go for it. Don't worry about what others think or say about you.

Think about all the cool stuff we have to eat. Have you ever wondered where some of these things came from? Think about chocolate. I love chocolate—especially the dark stuff—in all shapes, sizes, and forms. Everything from candy bars to chocolate drinks to ice cream.

Did you know that the chocolate we eat is the product of a long and delicate process that starts with the cacao tree? It grows in humid, tropical regions of the world. The cacao often grows in the shade of other trees, like the banana tree. The fruit of the cacao tree is a big pod with little beans inside it that grows right on the tree trunk. These beans are where we get chocolate from.

Gabi says:
Chocolate is the best! Whenever you feel sad, just eat a bar of chocolate—it will make you feel better.

I've always wondered who the first person was to taste a cacao bean. Was someone just out walking around one day, saw one of these big pods, cracked it open, and decided to munch on one? And how did the beans eventually make it from the pod to the candy we now enjoy? Trust me—it wasn't Willy Wonka! It took a bunch of people trying something new over and over again until it finally became edible—and enjoyable. I'm sure glad they weren't afraid to take risks to try something new. I can't imagine a world without chocolate!

Think about all the great inventors throughout history. Some of them failed hundreds—even thousands—of times before they were succesful with their invention. For example, take the Wright brothers. Orville and Wilbur Wright were born

> **Gabi says:**
> I'm glad someone took the risk to make chocolate! Without chocolate, we wouldn't survive!

in Ohio and grew up in a large family. They both became engineers and eventually started the Wright Cycle Company. While bicycles paid the bills, they were much more consumed with the idea of designing and constructing a heavier-than-air craft that would fly under its own power and under their control—an airplane as we know it today.

Orville and Wilbur began to experiment with kites, gliders, and other flying machines. Finally, on December 17, 1903, with Orville at the controls and Wilbur running alongside, they had the first manned, powered, and controlled flight in history in Kitty Hawk, North Carolina. They had to step out of their comfort zone, take a chance, and not worry about what other people thought. Am I ever glad they didn't give up on developing the first airplane! If it weren't for the Wright brothers, we'd be a lot less likely to explore places outside of our home state!

We take for granted a lot of the things that make life enjoyable, and we forget that someone had to try something new to start with. Think about life without electricity, refrigerators, computers, movies, cell phones, cold medicine—we have all this and much more because someone was willing to take a chance.

How about you? What are you missing out on in your life because you're afraid of taking a chance and trying something new? You might be surprised if you thought about it.

> **Gabi says:**
> If you really try to make an effort for something, you will succeed.

THE START OF SOMETHING NEW—FOR YOU

Are you afraid of trying new things?

Don't worry—you're not the only one who's ever been afraid to fail or be rejected. I don't like to admit it, but ever since my "shower experience," I still sometimes deal with the fear factor of trying new things. But I've also realized that there are lots of cool things in life to experience—from eating different kinds of food to making new friends—that I don't want to miss out on.

We shouldn't hold ourselves back from trying new things or meeting new people because of what others might think or because of our own self-doubts. We need to have confidence to take a chance. It means believing in yourself and your abilities. But where does this kind of faith come from? Let's check out some wise advice from a book that's been read by more people than any other in history—the Bible.

In Hebrews 11 there's a list of men and women who accomplished some incredible things. They took chances, stepped out of their comfort zones, and tried new things. In the process of taking risks, they impacted lots of other people and, in some cases, entire nations. How? By faith. It's faith that can give you the confidence to try something new. Hebrews 11:1 says this:

> Faith is the confidence that what we hope for will actually happen; it gives us assurance about things we cannot see.

Do you remember when you were real small and Christmas was just a few days away? You were eager and excited. You knew for sure you would get presents. But you also knew there would be some special surprises. Christmas is a lot like faith—it combines assurance and anticipation. But this kind of confidence is based on your past experience with God.

If we want to have confidence that helps us take risks and try new things, we have to trust God and believe in His promises to help us. Here's a verse that applies to what we've been talking about:

> For I can do everything through Christ, who gives me strength. Philippians 4:13

God doesn't make us superheroes and give us superhuman strength to do anything we can imagine, but He does give us the power to face the tough situations that can happen in life.

What's something new that you've been afraid of trying? Making new friends? Learning to play a sport or a musical instrument? Singing or acting? Wearing your hair a different way? Cooking?

Try something really new and ask God to help you. Don't be afraid of failing. Remember, anything can happen when you take a chance—especially when you have faith in God.

Gabi says:
At first playing my clarinet was really hard, but once I got into it, I started liking it. My band teacher helps make playing the clarinet fun. Remember, when you start to do something and it's hard, never give up.

KEEPING YOUR HEAD AND YOUR HEART IN THE GAME (OF LIFE)

If you're like other people your age, there are lots of possibilities in your life if you just look around. But you have to start somewhere, and usually it's easier to start with something simple before you move on to the big stuff.

This next week try some new things like:

→ Eat something different for breakfast.

→ Wear an outfit you haven't worn before; don't wear your favorite hat or pair of shoes this week.

→ Listen to a different style of music.

→ Introduce yourself to a new person at school.

→ Walk or drive a different way to school.

→ Change the order of your daily routine.

→ Comb your hair a different way.

It's a lot easier to try something new that's small than to try to accomplish some huge deal right away. But once you've accomplished some of the small stuff, it's time to move on to something bigger. How about trying out for a part in the school drama production? Or what about a position on a sports team at school? How about joining a club at school or learning how to play an instrument? Maybe you can talk with one of the leaders in your youth group and find out if there's a ministry at church where you could help out, like working with the children's ministry.

Think about the future. What dream do you have for your life? What can you do right now to start pursuing it? Don't forget the power you have available through Jesus. Without His help you won't be able to graduate to the bigger stuff.

As you learn to become a risk-taker, remember to let go and trust God. Trusting God is not a crutch; it's childlike confidence we put in Him. It's being willing to believe that God is able to do what He promises.

Is it hard for you to trust God? Why? What areas of your life do you need to trust God with? Slowly read the following verse and think about how it applies to you:

> Trust in the Lord with all your heart; do not de-
> pend on your own understanding. Seek his will in
> all you do, and he will show you which path to take.
> Proverbs 3:5-6

We must learn to trust God completely in every choice we make—believing that He knows what's best for us. And we must be willing to listen to and be guided by what's in God's Word.

THE BIG GAME

One of my favorite scenes in *High School Musical* is when Troy and the rest of the basketball team are doing some trick dribbling in the East High gym. There is some very cool stuff happening—the dancing and the ball handling. But Troy seems to be having trouble concentrating on basketball right now. His attention isn't on the game, it's on a girl—Gabriella. It's not love yet, but it's definitely infatuation. And then there's the song he can't get out of his heart and head. He's got an earworm!

What's gonna happen when Coach—his dad—and the rest of the team find out Troy's secret? Yikes! The Wildcats team captain sings? He's gonna have some tough explaining to do once the guys find out. But more than that—right now he

Gabi says:
Ooh...somebody's falling in love!

needs to focus and get his concentration back on basketball. Troy's gotta keep his head in the game if he's going to be able to "shoot the outside J" and help the team win the upcoming championship.

His body might be physically in the gym for practice, but Troy's having trouble with his head and heart. He's oblivious to the rest of the team ganging up on him, telling him to "get'cha head in the game." One minute he's talking about "grabbin and goin'," and the next Troy's hoping to "hit the right note." Wait a minute—what's up with this? He's gotta focus. Now his passion has a distraction—a pretty one—that's tugging at his heart. Should he go for it? Better shake it instead. Somehow Troy's got to focus on what's important right now—the game, not the girl—because it's affecting his game. He needs priorities—fast—to focus.

> **Gabi says:**
> Get that girl off your mind, Troy...or there's gonna be trouble!

OVERLOAD

We live in a sensory-overload world! Just look around you...it seems like every direction you turn there's something begging for your attention. You go online and get hit by pop-ups one after another. Then a friend wants to IM you. But wait a minute—now your cell phone is beeping because you have a new voice mail or text message. Turn on the TV and you get bombarded with a bunch of commercials. But hang on—you can always channel surf with the remote to avoid the ads. What about the billboards, bumper stickers, and posters? Did you know that we are exposed to hundreds of ads every day? There are so many that oftentimes we don't even notice the advertisements surrounding us.

At school there are more distractions. But when you're at home, everything gets even more complicated. You have homework, but your parents want you to clean your room and do your chores and your friends want you to hang out. Yikes! How are you supposed to concentrate? But wait a minute—you should be able to multitask anyway—shouldn't you? It's hard to stay focused on what's really important in the "big game of life" when there are so many temptations and distractions coming at you from so many different directions.

Gabi says:

It's bad for the brain having so many complicated things on your mind. It can make it hard to concentrate at school and at home.

Remember what Sharpay did right in the middle of the song "Stick to the Status Quo"? She screamed, "Everybody quiet!" Have you ever felt like doing that when your life seems overloaded and out of control? I have. Sometimes I feel like I'm on a treadmill in the middle of a blizzard and I can't get off!

WAIT A MINUTE

Throughout the year, when I speak in assemblies on public school campuses, I start each assembly with a drum solo. This definitely gets kids' attention and has earned me the nickname of "Drummer Dude." After performing a solo that includes playing not only the drums but anything else nearby—walls, chairs, microphone stands—I talk about making better choices in life. The main theme is "How You Choose to Live Today Will Determine How You Live Tomorrow," and I give five ways to make better choices. It's all about choosing wisely and avoiding negative consequences. Have you discovered that life is a series of choices and consequences? You are a product today of the choices you've made in the past. And your future will be directly affected by the choices you are making today. The Bible puts it this way: "You will always harvest what you plant" (Galatians 6:7). So what kind of choices are you making?

You can't plant corn seeds and expect apples to grow. Duh…it doesn't take a brain surgeon to figure that one out. It's a natural law to harvest what we plant. And the same is true in other areas of life. For example, if you're always gossiping about others, you won't have many friends; if you never do your homework, you can forget about getting good grades. Every choice has a consequence. Sometimes the choices we make and the consequences of those choices can impact our life in a greater way than we ever imagined.

> **Gabi says:**
> If you just take five minutes every day to think about the choices that you're going to make, you might not get in trouble so much. And you also might ask yourself—is that really me?

If we don't learn to focus on what's really important and sort out our priorities, we will continue to get sidetracked by distractions and temptations. Now, these distractions aren't all

> **Gabi says:**
> Just like if you don't practice your band instrument every day, you might not get good at it and your teacher might get mad at you.

necessarily bad. There are times when we have to say no to something good so we can say yes to something even better.

Other times we have to say "wait a minute" because it's not the time or the place to do something. This means there will be times in life when we need to make a decision before we are faced with temptations or distractions. For example, it would be better to decide now that you will not abuse drugs and alcohol—before you are tempted by someone at school or a party. The best time to choose is before you have to make a decision. It takes self-control, willpower, and convictions. In the Old Testament book of Daniel, there's a great example of a young man who had all three.

IT'S ALL IN YOUR HEAD

Daniel and his friends were taken from their homes in Judah and exiled to a foreign land. They faced an uncertain future, but they had some strong personal traits that qualified them to work as servants in the king's palace. With this position also came the opportunity to dine at the king's table, eating and drinking his food. But Daniel had decided long before this that he would not compromise the good habits—priorities—he'd already established in his life (Daniel 1:8). He knew what was important. So Daniel carefully chose a simpler diet that he proved was healthier. Even though he was living in a foreign country, he wanted to please God in his physical and spiritual life.

The king was so impressed with Daniel's abilities that he was going to elevate him to a new position that would put Daniel over the entire empire. Daniel was responsible and trustworthy when it came to his new responsibilities. But some of the other leaders became jealous that this "foreigner" had passed them up to be put in charge, so they decided to find a way to take Daniel down. But the only thing they could come up with had to do with his relationship with God. So they tricked the king into writing a new law that people could not pray to anyone but the king for the next month. The punishment for breaking this law was extreme—being thrown into a den of lions (Daniel 6:7). These guys were totally serious about getting Daniel!

I guess you could say that Daniel kept his head in the game, because as soon as he

Gabi says:
That's really mean to do to somebody, trying to trick Daniel into not being obedient to God. Don't let your friends affect your relationship with God.

heard about the new law, he went straight home and did what he always did—talked with God. Daniel not only knew what was important, he had convictions about it. A conviction is different from a belief. A belief is something you will argue for—a conviction is something you will die for. It's something that is so important to you—a priority—that you do it consistently and you don't let anything get in the way. You stay focused. A priority in Daniel's life was prayer, and he wouldn't let anything—even a law with deadly consequences—distract him from it.

Gabi says:
That was a brave thing for Daniel to do. Sometimes it takes courage to do the right thing when it comes to your relationship with God.

You can probably guess what happened next. The jealous leaders went running to the king and squealed on Daniel. Shortly after being arrested, he was thrown into the lions' den. But not before the king told Daniel he hoped that his God would rescue him. Early the next morning the king hurried to the lion's den and yelled to Daniel (6:19–20). God had miraculously protected Daniel, proving that he was innocent. The king ordered that Daniel immediately be lifted from the den. There was not a scratch on his body because he had kept his head in the game and trusted God.

There's a constant battle going on between your head and your heart. And there's pressure between choosing what is right and what is easy. It takes self-control and willpower to stay focused. And you can't do it on your own. You need God's help. Because the Holy Spirit of God lives inside you, all the power you need to keep your head in the game is available to you. But it means learning to trust God and relying on Him for help. He will help you sort out your priorities and focus on what is really important in your life.

> **Gabi says:**
> God can do amazing things! Trust in Him and see what happens in your life.

IMPORTANT STUFF

Troy found himself in a situation that's pretty common for lots of people. He was having trouble concentrating on what was important at a specific time—basketball practice. It isn't that his friendship with Gabriella and singing weren't important; the problem was the time and place. When he was at practice, that needed to be his priority, and he needed to keep his head free from distractions. If he was singing with Gabriella, then that would become the priority.

Because things are never the same and are always changing, there are times when your priorities may need to be adjusted. In order to decide what your priorities are, you need to figure out what things are most important to you. It's easy to have confused priorities, especially if you let your heart get in front of your mind—feeling instead of thinking. So what is most important to you? Friends? Family? School?

Where is God in your list of priorities? I've heard a lot of people say that God should be number one in your life. That sounds good at first, but think about it. If He is number one, that means He could also slip into the number two or number three position. It's healthier to think about living your life for and like Jesus, having the attitude that says, "Jesus is the center of my life."

Gabi says:
It's always best to have God in the center of your life because He can help you with your problems and with your relationships with your friends and parents. Just think about what life would be without Him to turn to.

Another way to think about priorities is to look at your goals. What are some specific things that you really want to accomplish? Maybe you want to learn to play a musical instrument or a new sport—where does this fit in your priority list? Sometimes we have too many things that we want to accomplish, so we have to ask if a new goal is something that we must do, should do, or can do.

You also have to be able to have enough self-control to say no to something that could be a distraction. Let's say you need to look up something online for a homework assignment, but a friend keeps IMing you. Connecting with your friend isn't bad, but it can be a distraction if you're trying to get homework done. If homework is a priority, you have to either ignore your friend or send her a quick IM to tell her that you can't talk right now. Develop the willpower to know what is best to do and when to do it.

Gabi says:
One of my goals is to learn how to play the clarinet really well—it's the best!

It's also good to know what kinds of things easily distract you—even good things. If you're like me and love music, you have to figure out when listening to music is a distraction to you. There are some projects I work on that need a lot of concentration, so I know I can't listen to music when I work on them. But there are other projects that

Gabi says:
Just because you might think it's a small homework assignment, you could still easily get distracted by turning on the tunes, and then you won't get it done.

don't require as much brain focus, so I can turn on some tunes. Self-control and deciding in advance just like Daniel did are important with situations like these.

Once you figure out the important stuff in your life, you'll have an easier time of gettin' your head in the big game—of life!

KEEPING YOUR HEAD AND YOUR HEART IN THE GAME (OF LIFE)

Have you ever taken the time to write out a list of your goals? Now is a good time to make a list of the stuff you want to accomplish in your life and then put it in order of importance. Remember to be specific. You may also want to separate them into short-term and long-term goals. For example, spending fifteen minutes a day reading a book (other than for homework) or maybe practicing your musical instrument or sport for thirty minutes each day could be considered short-term goals. But becoming a veterinarian when you get older or developing a habit of reading your Bible each day would be long-term goals. Also make a separate list of your daily priorities. Spend some quality time—without distractions—to pray about your list. It may take a while to come up with it, but you'll be glad that you did.

Here's something you can try that's fun and will help you with prioritizing. You'll need to get a wide-mouth jar. Fill it with pea-sized rocks. Then find a half dozen larger rocks and try to fit them into the jar, too. The big rocks don't fit, do they? Now repeat the process, only this time start by putting the big rocks in first, and then put the small rocks in the jar. Notice how the small rocks fill in around the big rocks.

The jar represents one week of your time. The small rocks represent the less important things in life—activities you enjoy but which aren't necessarily priorities, like IMing with friends or checking out cool sites online, watching a DVD, playing a video game, or riding your skateboard. The big rocks are activities that you think are important—priorities like doing your homework, reading your Bible, cleaning your room, and doing your chores.

What we learn from this experiment is that we can accomplish a lot more if we put the "big rocks" in first—take care of the priorities to start with. The important activities don't get crowded out, but you still have room for the smaller things, too.

Who or what is filling up your week? Think about your goals and check out your priorities. What needs to be changed?

Get'cha head in the big game of life!

(3)

ALWAYS THERE BESIDE ME

Gabriella and Troy sneak into the back of East High's theater to the watch the auditions for the winter musical. Sharpay and Ryan steal the show with their special arrangement of the song "What I've Been Looking For." As the others who auditioned leave the stage, Ryan tries to encourage them to still be a part of the musical—even if they only attend. Kelsi tries to talk with Sharpay about how she originally envisioned this song she wrote being performed a lot slower. Sharpay quickly puts the young "Sondheim" in her place by reminding Kelsi how many productions she and her brother have starred in. Sharpay also makes it clear

> **Gabi says:**
> Sharpay's such a show-off! She needs to be a more caring person, and so should we.

to Kelsi how she and Ryan have lifted the musical she wrote out of obscurity.

Right after Ms. Darbus calls for anyone else who wants to try out, Gabriella quickly makes her way down the aisle in the theater with Troy right on her heels. Not only is Ms. Darbus surprised that Troy is volunteering to sing with Gabriella, but she reminds them both that "the theater waits for no one." Troy and Gabriella plead with Ms. Darbus to give them a chance, but she has her mind made up. After everyone else has left the theater, Troy and Gabriella make their way onto the stage to help Kelsi pick up the musical charts she's dropped after tripping on the side of the piano.

Gabi says:
Darbus was mean to not let Troy and Gabriella sing. It was unfair to them, but sometimes life isn't fair. When something isn't fair, we should just learn to deal with it.

As Troy helps Kelsi with her music, he also tries to encourage her about being the "playmaker" in the musical since, after all, she wrote it. Standing around the piano, with Kelsi playing "What I've Been Looking For," Troy and Gabriella sing the tune at the tempo it was originally intended to be. Little do they realize that Ms. Darbus is listening from right outside the theater. She gives Troy and Gabriella a callback and asks Kelsi to work with them on another song.

What?! Ryan and Sharpay are furious when they see the callbacks posted with their names *and* Troy's and Gabriella's. Sharpay can't believe what's happened, and Ryan thinks they're getting punk'd by Ashton Kutcher. It's time to do something about Troy and Gabriella, they decide. Hmm…a plan is brewing…but it will eventually backfire on Ryan and Sharpay.

SURPRISE!

Have you ever been surprised by someone you didn't realize was standing right beside you?

One of my favorite places on the planet to visit is San Francisco—the City by the Bay. I grew up in the Bay Area and I like to go back and visit every chance I get. It's a fun place to go, with a bunch of different stores and great places to eat. A must-stop is Ghirardelli's Chocolate Factory for a hot-fudge sundae! And if there's time, a ride on a cable car.

> **Gabi says:**
> I love Ghirardelli's ice-cream sundaes! Everyone needs to taste one!

If the weather's good, there are usually some fascinating street performers—singers, magicians, painters, and jugglers—to watch. There's one guy who cracks me up because he's so clever at what he does. He camouflages himself to look like a big green bush and plants himself on the sidewalk by the wharf. Along comes an unsuspecting person who stands right next to the "bush." In an instant the bush guy starts shaking the branches he's wearing and totally scares the person next to him—and sometimes others standing close by! He waits for the crowd to disappear, then starts the whole process over again with another "victim."

Gabi says:
This guy's really funny to watch! I hope I'm never one of those people who gets scared. Are you easily scared?

Unless you visit San Francisco someday, you'll probably never see the "bush guy." But there is Someone else who's always standing next to you that you should get to know and understand. His plan isn't to frighten you—but to encourage and help you. Believe it or not, He's always been right there with you—even though you couldn't see Him. Who am I talking about? God.

Just imagine: The God of the universe is always with you, no matter where you go or what you do. But there's a lot more to understand about God and His characteristics. For example, did you realize that He knows everything about you? Or that He's not only good for you, but He's good *to* you? Talk about amazing—and there's more! You can't even imagine all that God wants you to experience. It's a feeling like no other!

WHAT'S HE REALLY LIKE?

I talk with people all the time who have some pretty strange ideas about what they think God is really like. How do you describe God? What do other kids at school say God is like? When I speak on public school campuses, I hear kids say things like God is dead or He doesn't really care about us. There are so many misconceptions that people have about God today.

Gabi says:
It's sad when you don't have a real relationship with God. He is the only one who can forgive your sins and make you a new person. He also helps you with your problems and gives you wisdom to make good decisions.

Some think God is like a police officer in the cosmos somewhere who wants to ruin your fun. Or how about the "nice old man God" who just sits around because He's too old and tired to do much of anything? Then there's the "hospital emergency room God," who is there when you get into real trouble, but for the everyday normal stuff, you don't mess with Him. Stop! This is so far from the truth about what God is really like. But unfortunately, this is what lots of people believe. You can be wrong about a lot of things in life, but you don't want to be wrong about God.

Let's take a look at how the Bible describes Him. A great place to start is in the book of Psalms—that's just about in the middle of the Bible. Check this out from Psalm 139:1–16:

> O Lord, you have examined my heart and know everything about me.
> You know when I sit down or stand up. You know my thoughts even when I'm far away.
> You see me when I travel and when I rest at home. You know everything I do.
> You know what I am going to say even before I say it, Lord.
> You go before me and follow me. You place your hand of blessing on my head.
> Such knowledge is too wonderful for me, too great for me to understand!
> I can never escape from your Spirit! I can never get away from your presence!

If I go up to heaven, you are there; if I go down to the grave, you are there.

If I ride the wings of the morning, if I dwell by the farthest oceans, even there your hand will guide me, and your strength will support me.

I could ask the darkness to hide me and the light around me to become night—but even in darkness I cannot hide from you. To you the night shines as bright as day. Darkness and light are the same to you.

You made all the delicate, inner parts of my body and knit me together in my mother's womb.

Thank you for making me so wonderfully complex! Your workmanship is marvelous—how well I know it.

You watched me as I was being formed in utter seclusion, as I was woven together in the dark of the womb.

You saw me before I was born. Every day of my life was recorded in your book. Every moment was laid out before a single day had passed.

Awesome! Let's unpack some of the things we just read, because there's a lot here that can affect your life.

Gabi says:

It's amazing what God knows about you! He knows everything you're thinking, what makes you happy and sad. He also knows your secrets—including your fears and what hurts you. So you can trust Him with everything in your life.

MORE THAN A KNOW-IT-ALL

Have you ever met somebody who thinks they know everything about everything? These people really bug me. I always want to find some crazy topic to discuss that they have no clue about—just to prove they really don't know it all.

Gabi says:
Some people can be real show-offs—just like Sharpay!

Sometimes we don't want people to get to know us very well because we're afraid they will find out something about us they don't like.

But God already knows everything about us—and He still loves us! Did you notice in the verses from Psalm 139 that God knows everything about you? He knows when you sit or stand; what you're thinking and feeling; even what you're going to say before the words come out of your mouth! It sounds crazy, but the Bible says God even knows the number of hairs on your head (see Matthew 10:30).

Gabi says:
Isn't that amazing? God knows the number of hairs on your head—even if you lose one! And if you're like me, you lose them all the time. Just look at your hairbrush!

God's knowledge is perfect about the stuff in your life that's happened in the past, the stuff that's going on right now, and the stuff that will take place in the future. He's totally aware of everything that goes on in your life (see Hebrews 4:13). Nothing escapes Him. Once you realize just how much God does know, it can make you feel either uncomfortable or very happy. Maybe you don't like the fact that God knows everything about you. It could be because you're doing some stuff that you shouldn't be doing. But just because you don't like the idea that God knows what's going on doesn't change the fact that He does. Maybe He wants to help you change these things.

Once you start to understand how well God knows you, it should give you confidence. There's never been anyone in your life who knows you like God does. He knows you better than you know yourself. God understands what scares you; He knows the hurt you may be experiencing; and He's aware of the trouble you may be having getting along with your parents or a friend. God understands everything you're going through, and He has answers to the

Gabi says:
God even has a plan for your life in the future. It's a good plan even though there will be ups and downs. Your life will be filled with exciting things when you follow God.

questions and problems in your life. After you learn this about God, it should cause you to respect and trust Him even more.

Maybe you need answers for a decision you have to make or a problem you're having—so pray and ask God for help. He will always answer you. But remember, it may take longer than you expect it to, or it may not be the answer you wanted. Keep in mind that God will always do what is best for you.

NEVER ALONE

Have you ever noticed how you can be in a large crowd of people and still feel terribly alone? Or if you've had the opportunity to travel much, being in a strange place can make you feel lonely, too—for friends, favorite foods, and familiar surroundings. Wouldn't it be great if you could always have someone beside you? You can and you do. Check out the verses we read earlier from Psalm 139. No matter where you go—from the depths of the ocean to the outer reaches of the heavens—God is always right there with us. He is present everywhere. You cannot escape from His Spirit. This is huge!

Remember when you used to play hide-and-seek? One person hides her eyes while counting to a certain number, then stops and yells, "Ready or not, here I come!" In the meantime, everyone else has attempted to hide someplace where they hope they won't be found. Sometimes we want to play hide-and-seek from God. Usually it's because we're involved in something that we shouldn't be or because God wants us to do something and we don't want to obey Him. This is a really dumb game to play with God.

Gabi says:
Jesus, your Savior, is always right beside you. So when you need Him, just put out your hand and He'll be there to lead you the right way.

There was a guy in the Bible named Jonah who tried to play this game. He learned the hard way that you can't run from God.

Jonah was given the task of going to a great evil empire—Assyria—to tell the people there about God's love and forgiveness. But Jonah hated the Assyrians, and instead of obeying God, he took off running in the

Gabi says:
Remember Jonah? He got into a fishy jam! God sometimes uses sticky situations to get our attention so we'll listen to Him.

opposite direction. He found a ship heading to a place called Tarshish, so he bought a ticket to escape from God.

The ship got caught in a violent storm, and when the sailors found out Jonah was running from God, they threw him overboard. Suddenly the storm stopped. God had arranged for Jonah to spend three days and nights inside the belly of a great fish to get his attention. When Jonah finally decided to obey God, the fish spit Jonah out onto the beach. Yech! Can you imagine how he smelled and looked?

Don't be a Jonah. Learn to trust and obey God—don't try to run from Him. Being present everywhere is part of God's care and protective plan for us. This is good news to those who know and love God, because it means that no matter what you do or where you go, you can never be far from God's presence.

Do you feel lonely at home or at school? Ask God to help you to know and feel that He's with you all the time. Maybe you're worried about someone hurting you—just remember that God is always with you no matter where you go. I've been in some pretty scary places in different parts of the world, and it always encourages me to know that I never go alone because God is always there with me.

REAL POWER

Lots of people I meet today are looking for power. They want power to change their lives, to feel special, and sometimes even to get vengeance on others who have hurt them. You should hear about some of the crazy places people look and the things they do to try to get power. But God is the only source of real power—the kind we need to change our lives.

You can't totally understand what God is like until you begin to grasp how awesome His power is. Not only is God all-powerful, but His power is also infinite, limitless. Look at what He did in Genesis, the first book of the Bible. In chapter 1 it tells how God spoke things into existence. That is amazing! Have you ever tried to speak something into existence? I love Italian food. I could try for days to point at a table and say "sausage, olive, and mushroom pizza," but no matter how hard I tried, it would never happen. Why? Because only God has the power to create something out of nothing. It's God's power that keeps the earth in perfect rotation around the sun. Any closer and we'd all be crispy critters; any farther away and we'd be Popsicles.

The Bible is filled with examples of how powerful God is. We read not only about His power to create but also about

His power over nature when He parted the Red Sea or calmed a storm. God healed the sick and gave sight to the blind; He even raised people from the dead! And the awesome thing is that God's power is the same today as it was when He created the planets and stars, and it will be the same ten thousand years from now! God's power never runs out, and it's available to us whenever we need it.

Gabi says:
God is powerful, so you don't want to mess with Him. Instead you want to ask Him for help.

When you get discouraged or don't feel very good about yourself, just remember that God made you. Just like we read earlier from Psalm 139, God created all our delicate parts. We are His workmanship, and God doesn't make any junk! His Spirit lives inside you, and God's power will help you to become the person He created you to be.

What do you need God's power for in your life today? Maybe your parents are getting a divorce and you don't know how you will get through this tough time; ask God to give you courage and strength. Or maybe you've developed a bad habit and you want to stop; God will help you if you ask Him and follow His guidance. Remember, there is no problem too small—or too big—for God.

KEEPING YOUR HEAD AND YOUR HEART IN THE GAME (OF LIFE)

Have you ever been rappelling? Basically, you lower yourself down a rock or the side of a cliff using a long rope. I vividly remember my first time. The friends I went with kept telling me to "trust the equipment." That was easy for them to say—I was the one hanging by a big rope attached to a harness around my waist and between my legs like a diaper. Needless to say, it wasn't something I was excited about wearing! But my friends were right about the equipment, because I didn't fall!

The hardest part for me was taking the first step off the top of this big eighty-five-foot-high rock we were rappelling down. After the first step, the rest of my rappelling adventure was awesome!

Sometimes it's hard to trust—especially when you've had a bad experience in the past. And the first step is usually the hardest. So who do you trust? God wants you to trust Him—to believe that He is always with you and will take care of you. God wants us to trust in his unfailing love for us (Psalm 13:5) and commit our plans to Him. Check out this promise in Proverbs 16:3. "Commit your actions to the Lord and your plans will succeed."

What areas of your life do you need to trust God with: your future, your friends, your family situation, your grades? God is trustworthy. You can depend on Him! But remember, it's hard to trust someone you don't know. Make sure you are spending some quality time growing in your relationship with Jesus by praying and reading the Bible consistently.

Take the first step, and Jesus will be right there beside you to help with whatever situation you are facing.

A SECRET I NEED TO SHARE

S trange things have been happening at East High ever since Troy and Gabriella made the callbacks for the musical. It's like everybody has a secret to share that doesn't fit with who they're supposed to be.

Zeke gets nothing but net on the basketball court. But he also likes to bake all kinds of things, including strudels, scones, and crème brûlée. The rest of the jocks are telling him not to "mess with the flow."

Martha Cox is a picture of extreme intelligence, but there's something about her that no one else knows—her secret obsession is hip-hop. She loves to "pop and lock and jam and break." But wait a minute—are brainiacs even supposed to do that? The brainiac crowd reminds Martha to "stick with what she knows."

What's happening to everyone? Now a skater dude opens up with a secret that he can't hide anymore—he plays the cello! (It's like a giant violin.) The crowd of dudes and dudettes tell the skater dude to "stick with the status quo."

Sharpay is stressed because she doesn't understand what's happening to everyone. This isn't the way she planned for things to go. She and Ryan know something is really wrong, and they gotta get things back to normal. People should stick with their group and the identity they have there. No one's supposed to try to break out of the mold they're in.

> **Gabi says:**
> Why can't people just be themselves? The real you is always better than the phony one.

The pressure's on to stick with the status quo and not to mess with the way things are. The way to be cool is to stick to this rule. But somehow things keep getting worse. Gabriella's chili fries get launched from her tray as she slips, and they end up on Sharpay. She tries to convince Ms. Darbus that Gabriella did it on purpose, as part of her plan to ruin the musical. Sharpay is also convinced "Troy and his basketball robots" are behind the plan, as well. Why can't everyone just stick with the stuff they know?

BRAINIACS, SKATERS, JOCKS, AND YOU

What group do you hang with? Everyone wants to fit in—feel like they're accepted and important. We all want and need relationships. So what's your group like? Do you treat others the way you want to be treated?

Every generation seems to have its cliques, clans, or tribes. There's significance and security in belonging to a small, exclusive group of people who share the same interests we do. Whether we belong to a subculture like goths, boarders, digit-heads, jocks, rappers, or even a drama group, we're all concerned about where and how we fit in.

But there's a huge downside to these groups. For example, think about how belonging to a group might give you a certain position or status. How about when the desire to be accepted motivates you to do almost anything? Or when you identify so much with a group that your own individual identity becomes a secret that no one knows.

Have you noticed how feeling secure is short-lived in these groups? You last only as long as you don't mess with the flow. These groups can also easily become judgmental and cruel. People get rejected because of the wrong standards, and sometimes things can even get violent.

There's nothing wrong with having a small group of close friends. God designed us as social beings—we need to be around other people. Sometimes He uses others to help get us through tough times. But God is totally against the abuse and misuse of friendships. That's why it is important to check out what the Bible says about friendship. Jesus is a great example of how we should treat others—inside and outside of our groups. He wasn't trying to look important, and He was always taking heat for spending time with misfits. Check out what happened one time:

> As Jesus was walking along, he saw a man named Matthew sitting at his tax collector's booth. "Follow me and be my disciple," Jesus said to him. So Matthew got up and followed him. Later Matthew invited Jesus and his disciples to his home as dinner guests, along with many tax collectors and other disreputable sinners. But when the Pharisees saw this, they asked the disciples, "Why does your teacher eat with such scum?" Matthew 9:9–11.

Jesus wasn't concerned with being accepted; instead, He wanted to do what was right by God's standards. He didn't play favorites or isolate himself from those who didn't fit in. Did you notice how in this story Jesus actually hurt His reputation with religious leaders by hanging out with Matthew and the other tax collectors? We should follow His example and not be afraid to be with others who may not fit in with our close friends.

The Bible has some strong things to say about playing favorites and ignoring others. Take

Gabi says:
You shouldn't just hang out with your group of friends. You should break out of your shell and spend time with new people because lots of people sit around all day with no one to talk to and have no one who cares.

a look at James, chapter 2. People were having problems with cliques, certain standards of money, and clothes when this part of the Bible was written. Check out verses 2–4 in this chapter:

> For example, suppose someone comes into your meeting dressed in fancy clothes and expensive jewelry, and another comes in who is poor and dressed in dirty clothes. If you give special attention and a good seat to the rich person, but you say to the poor one, "You can stand over there, or else sit on the floor"—well, doesn't this discrimination show that your judgments are guided by evil motives?

Think about it. Are we really any different today? Are you caught in this kind of trap? The Bible uses some strong language because it's important to God that we accept others no matter what they are and what they possess. But sometimes it's hard to do the right thing when there's pressure to stick with the status quo.

THE PRESSURE TO CONFORM

Have you noticed there seem to be some unwritten rules for membership in cliques, clans, and tribes? See if you can relate to these:

- You only hang around with members of your group.
- You are supposed to conform to be like everyone else.
- To be accepted you have to impress the unofficial leader of the group.
- You can't ever reveal your true feelings about anything until you know what the "group" thinks.

> **Gabi says:**
> Don't judge people by their appearance. Judge them by what really counts—what's on the inside—because God looks at the heart, and so should we.

Remember when Chad talks to Troy about all the crazy stuff that is happening? Not only is the team supposedly falling apart because of Troy's singing, but the brainiacs and drama geeks now think they have the right to talk with the jocks. And the skater dudes are mingling with other groups. All of a sudden people think they can do stuff that's not their stuff.

Peer pressure can be a huge influence in your life. It's the pressure we get from those around us to think like them. It can impact the way we think about ourselves, our parents, what's right and wrong—it even affects what we say and do. This pressure to conform to the values of others can be positive, but it's usually negative. It's all about acceptance.

How far would you go to be accepted by a group? Do you take your direction from the outside (others) or from inside (yourself)?

Maybe you've become like a chameleon. In order to survive, this lizard-type creature has the ability to change its color to adapt to its surroundings and hide from its enemies. Have you ever found yourself acting a certain way, talking a certain way, and even wearing certain clothes just to fit in with those around you?

You don't have to be a chameleon. When you use the Bible as a lens to look at how to live your life, you will see that God wants you to be *inner* directed. This happens when you develop a set of personal ideas to live by based on God's Word. You also need to know, understand, and guard your identity—who you are. Remember, you are who you choose to be.

Just like with all the Wildcats—who says you can't play basketball *and* sing? Or skateboard *and* play the cello? Or be a brainiac *and* like to hip-hop?

Be careful who you choose as friends and how much you allow them to influence you. You may have to choose some new friends if the ones you currently have are not a good influence on you. This is never easy to do, but think about the long-term effects on your life.

And guard against the fear factor—it's not a good position to be in. Check out what the Bible says:

> Fearing people is a dangerous trap, but trusting the Lord means safety. Proverbs 29:25

When you're afraid of others it can hold you back from accomplishing things, and it can keep you from being who you really are. It's better to trust God and do what pleases Him. Remember, He's the one who made you and who knows what's best.

When you're inner directed, you will be able to stand up to the pressure to conform and do what is right rather than what seems easy and convenient. We should never get tired of doing what's good and right (see 2 Thessalonians 3:13).

The real problem is that temptation from others doesn't usually start with doing some huge, awful thing. It's often something small that builds gradually, and before you know it, you look back and can't figure out how you ended up where you are. I've had the opportunity to speak to girls and guys in a lot of juvenile jail facilities. I've lost track of the number of times I've heard someone say they didn't realize what was happening—it was so subtle. But they were with the wrong group of people at the wrong time, and that's how they got busted.

Chances are you'll never have to worry about getting busted, but you may end up in a self-imposed prison because of the pressure of friends. Don't let others keep you from your passion and from being the person God designed you to be.

> **Gabi says:**
> If your real passion is art, but you hang out with the wrong group that gets in trouble, there could be a consequence. You may not be able to follow your dream of being an artist.

WHAT'S YOUR SECRET OBSESSION?

Every person has been created with a combination of gifts, talents, and abilities that are unique to him or her. Even identical twins are not wired the same exact way. God gives us these talents and abilities as well as the wisdom to know how to use them (see Exodus 28:3).

As we explore these abilities, we become passionate about certain ones that we really like doing. Like the skater dude said, "There's no explanation for the awesome sensation" we get from our secret obsessions. And these things may change as we get older.

I had a secret obsession that very few people ever knew about until now. Promise me you won't laugh. When I was about six or seven years old, I tap-danced.

> Gabi says:
> LOL!!!

Believe it or not, I was actually on a weekly TV show on a local channel in the San Francisco Bay Area. My aunt was a very accomplished dancer and had her own dance studio and TV program. Nobody can imagine me—the drummer dude—tap-dancing my way across the stage and screen. Yet it was my sense of timing and rhythm that enabled me to dance and eventually play drums. The truth is that I liked tap-dancing—but I never told anyone because I was afraid of what they would say. It was a trap I fell into because of fear. I've learned how wrong it was to be afraid and that even if my friends did laugh—and I can't blame them with this one—that I would have been okay.

What's your secret obsession? Whether it's cooking, singing, dancing—whatever it is—go for it! Think about your special tal-

> **Gabi says:**
> I never knew that my great aunt had a dance studio! Next time I see her I will have to tell her that I've taken ballet, tap, and jazz.

ents and abilities and the ways you could use them for God's work in the world. Be an example for your friends. Don't let anyone rob you of the fun you can have by following your passion. You can be proud of these talents and abilities—no matter what they are. It's all right to step away from the crowd to be you. But it's also important that we support one another. Go ahead and mess with the flow. Don't settle for the status quo!

> **Gabi says:**
> Just be yourself and don't worry about what other people think! Being yourself is what really counts to God and to others.

KEEPING YOUR HEAD AND YOUR HEART IN THE GAME (OF LIFE)

Be careful about giving in to the temptation to stick with the status quo. Here's a great promise to remember from the Bible:

The temptations in your life are no different from what others experience. And God is faithful. He will not allow the temptation to be more than you can stand. When you are tempted, he will show you a way out so that you can endure. 1 Corinthians 10:13

Just remember to ask for God's help and surround yourself with friends who will encourage you to do the right thing and be the best you can be.

Take some time this week to thank God for making you unique and different from everybody else. Stop comparing yourself to others and society's standards. Think about the talents and abilities you have been given. What are some new ways you can use them to help others? Write down your ideas and ask God to give you wisdom to make these things happen.

Learn to accept others just the way they are—with their strengths and weaknesses. Let your friends know that it's safe to share their secret obsessions with you. Then make sure you encourage them to keep using their talents and abilities. We need to celebrate the variety that is in each of our lives. It will make the world a better place to live in.

5

HEARTBREAKER

Troy's in trouble with his teammates and his dad—the coach—when he starts putting more energy and attention into singing in the school musical than basketball. The big concern is the possibility of getting their "sorry butts kicked" in the championship game that's only two weeks away. At the same time Taylor and the scholastic decathlon team plead with Gabriella to focus on their upcoming competition instead of the winter musical. Chad and the basketball team, along with Taylor and the scholastic decathlon team, have devised a plan to split up Troy and Gabriella.

Chad and the team take Troy on a trip down memory lane with previous Wildcat legends—including his own father—to convince him how important he is to the team. They keep reminding him to "get his head in the game."

Troy reminds his guys, "If you don't know that I'll put 110 percent of my guts in that game, then you really don't know me." Meanwhile, Taylor and her team are trash-talking Troy, "the lunkhead basketball man," and they remind Gabriella that their side is "the future of civilization." Gabriella pretty much ignores them until she sees and hears Troy—via a hidden Web cam in the boys' locker room—reminding the other guys that he's all for the team and that singing is no big deal. It's just a thing he does to keep his nerves in check. Troy makes it clear that Gabriella isn't important to him. "I'll forget about her. I'll forget about the audition and we'll go out and get that championship."

> **Gabi says:**
> It's kind of mean that Chad and Taylor are setting their friends up. We need to be careful about not hurting others.

Troy's words were mean and really hurt Gabriella's feelings. Heartbroken, she tells Troy she's done with him and singing. "You've got your team and I've got mine," she says. At first Troy can't understand what's up with Gabriella's snubbing him. He decides to give up on her and singing until Chad confesses what he and Taylor have done. Now it's time for Troy to apologize to Gabriella and win her back.

ME AND YOU

Have you ever found yourself looking in from the outside after someone said something really mean to you? With this person or situation, did you feel like you confused your feelings with the truth? Or maybe you were the one whose words hurt someone else. That was me as a teenager. My mouth should have been declared a lethal weapon—especially when it came to girls. Don't get me wrong—I liked girls. I just didn't think they could like me because of the way I looked. I hated myself because of it. I was too tall and skinny and had two fangs sticking out of my mouth—kind of a vampire thing. On top of my head was dark curly hair, which I hated because I wanted straight blond hair. But the worst part of all was my embarrassingly oversized nose. I think my mom gave birth to a five-pound nose and my body grew off it!

Gabi says:
Lots of laughter!
Sometimes I think
my dad is crazy!

Consequently I didn't think anyone could like me unless I was sitting behind a set of drums. And strange as it sounds, when it came to girls, my goal in life was to see how quickly I could make them cry. I said some pretty cruel things, just like Troy did to Gabriella. In high school I really liked a girl named Karen. She was very pretty with big brown eyes, dark brown hair, and a cute smile. One Saturday night my band was opening in concert for Santana—it was HUGE for us! We were totally excited as a band—and so were our girlfriends. All during the concert Karen was backstage with me. She kept bringing me stuff to eat and drink. After the show we were soaring and felt like we could reach up and touch the stars!

Karen was totally excited. "Steve, I'm so proud of you. I can hardly wait to show you off to everyone tonight when we all go out to eat." "Karen, you don't really expect me to go out with you looking like that. What's up with that outfit?" "What?! I bought this outfit special just for tonight." "Well, it would look better on a hanger than it does on you. And what's the deal with your hair—it looks like you stuck your finger in a light socket." "Please stop being so mean to me, Steve." I kept saying cruel things to Karen until she started to cry and left. It sounds sick now, but I actually felt like a big man. After all—I was the big-time rock drummer in the band—and I could make girls cry by being mean to them. But

Gabi says:
What in the world were you thinking? I can't believe you were so mean. She cared about you and was just trying to be nice.

here's the part I couldn't understand: Karen never would go out with me the rest of high school. And she'd hardly speak to me…. Go figure…girls….

A couple years after we graduated, Karen and I attended the marriage of a friend we both went to school with. "Steve," she said, "there was a time when I thought that you and I would one day get married. But I couldn't take your constant put-downs—why couldn't you have just been yourself instead of being so mean?" Just like Troy and Gabriella, I guess Karen's heart was empty once I changed the words.

Unfortunately, sometimes relationships just don't work. Whether people bully you at school or your best friend dumps you for no reason, or you get kicked out of a group you've been part of, you can see that relationships are sometimes fragile and painful. Healthy ones take work—but they're worth it.

> **Gabi says:**
> It's really good to have close friends, because when you have a problem or you're upset, you can go to them for help and advice. Make sure you're a good friend to others.

Lots of things can affect our relationships and how we treat others. Jealousy can be a huge problem; so can a poor self-image. I didn't like myself, and that's why I treated people—

especially girls—so awful. What's your excuse—or are you a victim? Miracles can happen in relationships if we approach them the right way.

RELATIONSHIPS THAT WORK

Let's be real. We all want relationships that work. Whether it's having friends we can rely on, having a group to hang with and have fun with, or eventually the guy-girl thing, they're all important and necessary. So how do we develop healthy relationships? Let's check out the Owner's Manual and see what God has to say about healthy friendships. There's a lot of good stuff that can really help us.

Start with how you choose your friends; it's more important than you think. Why? Because we become like those we spend the most time with. This can be a good thing or a not so good thing. Check out 1 Corinthians 15:33: "Bad company corrupts good character."

So who do you spend the most time with: people who encourage you to be the best you can be, or people who are always trying to get you to do or say things that you know aren't right? Now flip it around. What kind of friend are you? Do you think people will like you more if you're always at the center of all the "bad stuff" going on? Don't let your relationships lead you in the wrong direction. Also, make sure that you're a positive influence on others.

Friendship is a priceless gift from God, and He gives us a great example of it in the story of David and Jonathan. It's found in 1 Samuel 18:1–4:

Gabi says:
It's good to have healthy friendships. Good friends can help you when you're in a tough situation. They can cheer you up when you're sad, and they can warn you if you're making a bad choice and help you to make good ones.

> After David had finished talking with Saul, he met Jonathan, the king's son. There was an immediate bond of love between them, for Jonathan loved David. From that day on Saul kept David with him and wouldn't let him return home. And Jonathan made a solemn pact with David, because he loved him as he loved himself. Jonathan sealed the pact by taking off his robe and giving it to David, together with his tunic, sword, bow, and belt.

Right after they met, David and Jonathan became close friends. Have you ever had this happen to you? I have, and it's very cool. David and Jonathan's friendship is one of the closest you will find in the Bible. But here's something to think about: They based their friendship on God, not on each other. This enabled David and Jonathan not to let anything come between them. Even when their friendship was tested, it brought them closer together.

> **Gabi says:**
> Just like David and Jonathan, I have a close friend who is like a sister to me. We've known each other since we were both real little. I thank God for giving me her as a friend.

What do you base your relationships on, God or each other? Keep in mind, until you have a relationship with God first, your human friendships will be difficult. That's because our relationship with God affects every area of our lives, including the friends we have. Once you have decided to live for Jesus, you will be able to start having relationships that work with others.

How does God want us to treat our friends? There's some great advice found in Colossians 3:12–14 that can help us in our relationships with our friends and even our family members, too. It says this:

> Since God chose you to be the holy people he loves, you must clothe yourselves with tenderhearted mercy, kindness, humility, gentleness, and patience. Make allowance for each other's faults and forgive anyone who

offends you. Remember, the Lord forgave you, so you must forgive others. Above all, clothe yourselves with love, which binds us all together in perfect harmony.

God wants these qualities to be locked deep inside of us— not just on the surface, where things can change too easily. We need to be sensitive and kind to others. That means we do more than care about others—we put our caring into action and help them when we can. God wants us to have a right view of ourselves and to be humble—to put others first. We also need to be patient with others—which isn't always easy, especially when it comes to their faults and things we may not like about them. Just remember, no one is perfect; we all make mistakes. And we all expect other people to understand us, so we should be willing to do the same for them.

One of the hardest things God expects us to do is forgive others for what they've done to us. But it's the best thing we can do. Holding a grudge against someone is like putting ourselves in prison—we can't move on with our lives and it can cause us to be bitter.

Linking all these qualities for friendship together is love. But the kind of love the Bible is talking about is not based on feelings. It's a choice we make. No matter what may happen, we choose to continue to love our friends. The book of Proverbs reminds us that a friend loves at all times (see 17:17 NIV).

Do your best to practice these traits in your relationships with friends and family members. But remember, sometimes no matter how hard we try to work at a relationship, people will disappoint us. There's always a risk that some relationships may be painful. It seems to happen a lot today—especially when it comes to families breaking up.

Early one morning when I was a kid, my dad knocked on my bedroom door, came in, and sat down on the edge of my bed. "Son, I want you to know your mother and I are getting a divorce. We don't love each other anymore," he said. I was in shock. Instantly my stomach began to ache—it felt like it was tied up in knots. My brother, sister, and I knew my parents had been fighting a lot, but we never thought it would end in divorce. I asked Dad if it was something us kids had done that caused them to split up. But he reassured me that it had nothing to do with us and everything to do with them. Not long after that, my grandfather died. I'd never experienced so

> **Gabi says:**
> Whenever you're stuck in a situation like that, you should always turn to God for help. He will give you courage and strength.

much heartache before. I didn't know who to turn to or what to do to make the pain go away. And I was angry with God. Why was He allowing all this stuff to happen to me? Couldn't He do something to stop these things from happening?

Even though we may not understand why our parents split up or why someone we thought was our best friend dumped us, we can be sure of one thing: God will never let us down. He promises to always be there for us, no matter what happens.

> I will never fail you. I will never abandon you.
> Hebrews 13:5

This promise doesn't mean our lives will be without pain—unfortunately, that's part of life. Nothing that occurs in our lives, however, takes God by surprise, and He has a purpose for everything that happens to us. No matter what, God will always be there to help put the pieces of your broken heart back together again.

The most important relationship you will ever have is with God. Get to know Him by spending time each day reading the Bible and praying. The better you get to know Him, the more you will be able to trust Him. It's just like any other friendship—you have to spend time with someone to really get to know them. This is especially important when it comes to knowing God.

KEEPING YOUR HEAD AND YOUR HEART IN THE GAME (OF LIFE)

When it comes to any relationship, there's another principle that applies in every situation with every person. Whether it's a friend or family member, we should always treat others the way we want to be treated. Check out what Jesus said:

> Do to others whatever you would like them to do to you. This is the essence of all that is taught in the law and the prophets. Matthew 7:12

Some people have called this the "Golden Rule," and along with love, it is a main part of any relationship that works. When you're with others at home or at school, try to become more sensitive to how you talk and act toward them. Is this the way you would want to be treated? Take it one step further and do something nice for others as often as you can. You might be surprised at what happens with these acts of kindness, and it will definitely please God.

Doing something nice for someone else might be difficult to do if you haven't forgiven that person for something they did to you. As far as God is concerned, forgiving others is not optional. To forgive someone means to "let it go" and not expect anything from them in return. Think about it: What do we really accomplish by not forgiving someone? Unforgiveness harms us more than the person who has hurt us. Is there anybody in your life that you need to forgive? Ask God to help you "let it go"—whatever it was they did to hurt you—and move on with your life. If possible, tell this person that you forgive them and why. You'll be amazed at how much better you will feel and how learning to forgive can make a difference in your relationships.

6

SHOOTING
FOR THE STARS

Gabriella can't seem to concentrate on preparing for the upcoming decathlon meet, while Troy's basketball game goes down the tubes. He just can't make a shot. It's pretty obvious that neither one of them is acting normal. Everyone around them has noticed a huge change in Gabriella and Troy. They've lost their desire to compete and just seem to be going through the motions with their teams. Their hearts aren't in it anymore.

> **Gabi says:**
> If you don't follow your heart, you won't be yourself. Make sure your heart is where God wants it.

Gabriella is still hurt that Troy told his team that she and singing didn't really matter to him. Troy continues to be clueless that his teammates tricked him into saying mean things about Gabriella. Relationships can get so complicated!

Chad and Taylor—along with both teams—feel guilty for what they've done, and they finally admit it to Troy and Gabriella. Troy gets the word from his guys at his rooftop hideaway and can't believe how dumb they were to do such a crazy thing. He decides to make things right with Gabriella, so he goes to her house to apologize. It takes extreme effort on Troy's part to get Gabriella to listen—like climbing up to the second-floor porch outside her bedroom window! But his efforts pay off, and they both decide to sing together in the callbacks.

Gabi says:
Go Troy!

In the meantime, Ryan and Sharpay, co-captains of the drama club, have convinced Ms. Darbus to reschedule the callbacks at the same time as the championship basketball game and the decathlon competition. Their plan is to eliminate the competition—Troy and Gabriella. We'll see what happens to their plan in the next chapter.

The day of the callbacks finally arrives. The dynamic duo of Ryan and Sharpay wow the crowd with their cool outfits, dancing, and singing about climbing the ladder of success. They want to bop to the top by working their tails off and blowing the competition away.

Ms. Darbus is impressed—that's for sure. And since Troy and Gabriella haven't shown up yet, it looks like Sharpay and Ryan may have succeeded once again in grabbing the lead roles in the musical.

Gabi says:
This is my favorite song! I like it because it has a great beat and it encourages you to be the best you can be and go for your dreams.

DREAMIN'

What's your dream? Do you want to be the next *American Idol* winner? Or maybe you want to explore outer space. Perhaps you'd like to compete in extreme sports. Maybe acting is your passion and someday you want to walk down the red carpet at the Academy Awards.

If you could be anyone and do anything in the world, what would it be? Everyone has a dream and

Gabi says:
My dream is to become a veterinarian. I love animals and I want to help them.

wants to be successful. Most people I talk with think success equals happiness. But I discovered that's not always reality.

I grew up in the San Francisco Bay Area—northern California. From the time I was a really small guy, my dream was to be a professional drummer. My mom would tell you she knew I was going to be a drummer even before I was born. She worked as an administrative assistant in an office and remembers sitting at her desk typing on the keyboard while I would tap out rhythms in her stomach.... Moms...go figure!

> **Gabi says:**
> Grandma is a crazy lady. She even sings to her birds in the morning. But I love her anyway!

I was convinced the drums could give me everything I wanted in life: fame, money, expensive cars, and girls! My dream was to get to Southern California—Hollywood. I thought if I could achieve all these things, I'd be successful—and happy.

There were a couple of detours along the way, like when I tried to learn to play the piano and the clarinet. Let's just say I was pretty lame on both instruments!

> **Gabi says:**
> LOL! I can't imagine Dad trying to play the clarinet! It must have been funny to watch!

But when I reached seventh grade, drums became my passion. That's when I bought my original drum kit and started playing in my first band.

My success came at an early age. By the end of seventh grade, I was a pro. Our band was getting paid to play at parties, dances, and grand openings of stores. We were so professional that our moms thought we should have matching outfits.

> **Gabi says:**
> You remind me of the Target commercial! LOL.

I can't believe we used to play gigs wearing white shirts with big red polka dots all over them! We should have been called the Measles Boys!

High school meant new opportunities, including playing with older guys in night clubs on some weekends. I also played in a band with friends from school. We opened in concert for bands like Santana and Fleetwood Mac. It was awesome! My dream was starting to become a reality—I was making some serious dollars and had a cool car and a girlfriend. I knew that if I kept at it long enough, drums could give me the success, satisfaction, and happiness I wanted out of life.

I also used my drums as something to hide behind. I had a terrible self-image and hated the way I looked. I couldn't understand why God made me the way He did. In my mind I

> **Gabi says:**
> Dad was crazy to be thinking that. People should always like us for what's inside of us.

was convinced that no one could like me unless I was sitting behind a set of drums.

By the time I graduated from high school, my career was really taking off. I'd developed a solid reputation in the San Francisco Bay Area playing all kinds of gigs—from concerts to nightclubs to touring Broadway shows on the West Coast. In spite of all I had achieved, my dream was still to move to Hollywood to make it big in the music industry. Little did I realize what would happen in my life as I pursued my dream.

One day while I was buying some drum equipment at Allegro Music Store, the owners approached me about giving drum lessons. My first question was, "How much money does it pay?" You see, money was my god back then. I also told the store owners that I couldn't be there every week because of tour schedules and out-of-town gigs. That was cool with them. Within a week I started giving drum lessons at the store.

It was awesome! I was getting paid money to teach others how to play drums…and talk about how great I was. I had students as young as eight, and there was a man in his sixties taking lessons. Most of my students looked up to me and wanted to be just like me. But not Robbie, who was almost a teen. He knew I was a good drummer, but he spent more time talking about his best friend. And for some reason that really bugged me.

Every week he would come in for his lesson and tell me a different story about his best friend. At first what Robbie was saying sounded a little strange. I mean, he was with this friend all the time and said he could talk with him about anything. Soon I became jealous because I didn't have a friend like Robbie did. But I tried to be cool and not let Robbie know what I was thinking and feeling. After all, I was the "big time drummer" who was on the fast track to success. That was the first time I started to realize that maybe the success I had achieved so far wasn't satisfying.

Gabi says:
Dad really wanted a friend like this. Doesn't everybody?

I finally decided I wanted to know more about this friend of Robbie's. "Hey, Rob," I said as he was leaving his lesson. "I've been hearing you talk about your best friend week after week, but you've never told me his name. What is it?" I was not prepared for his answer. "Jesus," Robbie replied. I had no clue Robbie was talking about Jesus from the Bible. I thought he had this little Latino friend—Jesus Martinez or Jesus Alvarez.

Gabi says:
LOL! Why would Dad think that? Didn't he read his Bible back then?

"What's his last name?" I asked. "Christ," he answered. Then he pointed at me and said, "He can be your best friend, too!" Unbelievable! I was speechless! It was like my whole life stopped and I was in freeze-frame mode. A relationship with God? Maybe that was what I'd been searching for all that time.

It wasn't long after that when I met Robbie's uncle and aunt who were entertainers in Hollywood. Billy and Danielle were awesome and seemed to have everything I wanted out of life. They were talented, good-looking, and successful. Billy and Danielle soon offered me a gig with their band in Hollywood. They suggested that I drive down to Southern California with them between Christmas and New Year's so I could check out the situation with the potential gig.

Do you know what we talked about the entire drive from northern to Southern California? Their relationship with Jesus. This was huge! It was like I had waited my whole life to hear what they were saying. Billy and Danielle talked about how only Jesus could satisfy me. I would never be famous enough or have enough money (see 1 John 5:12). They helped me understand what sin was and how God demonstrated

His love for me by sacrificing
His Son, Jesus, on the cross
for me (see Romans 5:8). Billy
and Danielle also told me how

Gabi says:
Now, that's the kind
of best friend that
you need!

I could be part of God's forever family (see John 1:12). This
was huge for me because I came from a broken home. I had
a lot to think about.

We hit the ground running in Southern California, going
places and meeting with different people. It seemed pretty
weird, but in the midst of all the "business stuff" we were
doing, I wanted to know more about Jesus. By Thursday of
that week, I knew the real reason I was there: to establish a
personal relationship of my own with God. That very night
I made the decision to live my life for Jesus.

A few months later I joined Billy and Danielle's band and
moved to Southern California. This was it…I was on my way
to becoming a big-time rocker!

Many more opportunities came my way after I moved there.
We entertained some of the biggest stars of TV and movies.
There were other gigs entertaining pro athletes and race car
drivers. I went to parties where celebrities hung out—you
know, like the ones you read about and see on TV. I was so
caught up with the music biz, the "new" Steve got lost as I

Gabi says: Always make time for God in your busy day. Just five minutes reading the Bible and praying helps!

continued to pursue my dream. I didn't have time for God right then—I was shooting for the stars!

Then I received several different offers to play drums for some of the biggest names in music and entertainment. These opportunities were huge! More money than I had ever imagined making—and lots of awesome benefits. It was everything I had ever wanted.

But something wasn't right with these offers. Even though it was my dreams coming true, I couldn't take the gigs. You see, I was involved with another band at this time, one from Biola University, a Christian school in Southern California. On my off nights I was playing Christian concerts at churches, camps, and schools. God was using our music to tell people—especially youth—about having a relationship with Him. It was a strange place to be, like being trapped in two different worlds. Some guys even suggested that God wanted me in ministry. *Not a chance,* I thought. *I'm going to be a big-time rocker!*

But something was happening that I couldn't explain. I was changing. And for the first time in my self-centered Christian life, I decided to pray about these opportunities. It seemed like the things I always thought would satisfy me—the fame, money, cars, and girls—did not satisfy me and make me happy.

It was playing with the Christian band that gave me a real sense of satisfaction. God was using me to help others! And I kept remembering what Billy and Danielle had shared with me on the ride to Southern California—only Jesus can truly satisfy.

> **Gabi says:**
> That is so true! Jesus gives us purpose in our life, so we should serve Him.

I slowly began to realize that I had something the entertainment business couldn't offer. There was a difference between me and all the celebs I was hanging with. I had something they didn't have, and I didn't need their life to make me feel important and happy.

I never heard a voice from the cosmos or saw a message written across the sky, but I knew what I had to do. Finally, to the shock of my family and friends—and to myself, as well—I said no to these gigs. Everyone asked me what I was going to do, and I responded, "I'm not sure, but I think God wants me in ministry." I guess you could say I said no to rock 'n' roll so I could say yes to the solid rock.

> **Gabi says:**
> Good choice! Look at how God used you to help people.

You will have the same opportunity in the next chapter to say yes to the King of Kings by establishing a relationship with God. It's the key to satisfaction and happiness in life.

But there was a man who lived a long time ago—who was a lot smarter than I am—who went on a similar search and came to an amazing conclusion.

ADVICE FROM A WISE GUY

Almost three thousand years ago a man named Solomon talked about satisfaction and happiness in life. He might as well have written his insights today because they are totally relevant to our lives. What made Solomon so special was his wisdom. When he became king, he asked God for wisdom (see 2 Chronicles 1:7–12), and he became the wisest man in the world (see 1 Kings 4:29–34). Solomon studied, wrote, judged, and taught. People from all over the world traveled to Jerusalem to learn from him.

Solomon searched for satisfaction like a scientist conducts an experiment. Check out this account of what he did, found in Ecclesiastes 2:1–10:

I said to myself, "Come on, let's try pleasure. Let's look for the 'good things' in life." But I found that this, too, was meaningless. So I said, "Laughter is silly. What good does it do to seek pleasure?" After much thought, I decided to cheer myself with wine. And while still seeking wisdom, I clutched at foolishness. In this way, I tried to experience the only happiness most people find during their brief life in this world.

I also tried to find meaning by building huge homes for myself and by planting beautiful vineyards.

Gabi says:
Busy guy.

I made gardens and parks, filling them with all kinds of fruit trees. I built reservoirs to collect the water to irrigate my many flourishing groves. I bought slaves, both men and women, and others were born into my household. I also owned large herds and flocks, more than any of the kings who lived in Jerusalem before me. I collected great sums of silver and gold, the treasure of many kings and provinces. I hired wonderful singers, both men and women, and had many beautiful concubines. I had everything a man could desire!

So I became greater than all who have lived in Jerusalem before me, and my wisdom never failed me. Anything I wanted, I would take. I denied myself no pleasure. I even found great pleasure in hard work, a reward for all my labors.

STOP! This is huge. Can you imagine being Solomon? Sounds like a dream come true! This guy had it all; he denied himself nothing! Unbelievable! I mean, this had to satisfy him and make him happy, right? Wrong! Check out what Solomon says in the very next verse:

Gabi says:
He should have given some of that "meaningless stuff" to the poor! (Dad is laughing.)

But as I looked at everything I had worked so hard to accomplish, it was all so meaningless—like chasing the wind. There was nothing really worthwhile anywhere.

Huh? Was this guy nuts? How could he be that successful and have all that stuff and say it's meaningless? Remember, the Bible called him the wisest man in the world. So what did he find out that we need to know? Jump ahead to the last chapter of Ecclesiastes to see what Solomon concluded about the meaning of life.

> That's the whole story. Here now is my final conclusion: Fear God and obey his commands, for this is everyone's duty. Ecclesiastes 12:13

Solomon isn't saying it's wrong to dream and shoot for the stars. There is nothing wrong with wanting to be successful and happy, as long as we understand how to really achieve these things. Solomon found out from personal experience that you cannot find meaning in life through knowledge, money, pleasure, work, or popularity. The problem is the more we try to get, the more we realize how little we really have. There is no lasting satisfaction or happiness without God.

You can "bop to the top" as long as you remember a couple of things. First, true satisfaction comes from knowing that what you are doing is part of God's purpose for your life. Second, we need to understand the way to achieve happiness. Solomon concluded, "To the man who pleases him, God gives wisdom, knowledge and happiness" (Ecclesiastes 2:26 NIV). In other words, happiness is the result of obedience.

> **Gabi says:**
> That's totally true! We should always obey God because He gives true happiness in our lives. Don't let other things or other people distract you from doing what God wants you to do.

If we want to be happy, we need to do what pleases God and obey Him. It's not complicated, but it's not easy, either. It's going to take some effort on our part, and we need to trust God, recognizing that He knows what will satisfy us. After all, He created us. Ask God to help you—and He will.

KEEPING YOUR HEAD AND YOUR HEART IN THE GAME (OF LIFE)

Let's face it, no one wants to be a loser or be unhappy. It can be a very real fear—one that can be like a self-imposed prison. So how can we keep from falling into this trap and finding real happiness and satisfaction? Check out the advice David gave us in Psalm 27:1–3:

> The Lord is my light and my salvation—so why should I be afraid? The Lord is my fortress, protecting me from danger, so why should I tremble? When evil people come to devour me, when my enemies and foes attack me, they will stumble and fall. Though a mighty army surrounds me, my heart will not be afraid. Even if I am attacked, I will remain confident.

Fear can be a dark shadow that consumes us from within. When we're afraid of failing, we can actually defeat ourselves and not even realize it. But we can conquer the fear of failure—and any other fear—by trusting in the Lord. He will save us from stumbling and falling. And He will also show us the purpose He has for our life. But we have to trust Him and decide to do what pleases Him—obey Him by doing what He asks us to do.

How do we know what He wants us to do? The best way is by reading and studying His Word—the Bible. I like what James 1:22 says about being doers of the word:

> But don't just listen to God's word. You must do what it says. Otherwise, you are only fooling yourselves.

It's certainly important to listen to God's Word at church, in youth group, or even on podcasts. But it's way more important to apply it to your life and do what it says. And don't forget the connection Solomon made between obeying God and happiness. You can't have one without the other.

Is there something that God has been asking you to do lately that you keep ignoring? Maybe it's time for an attitude check.

······························(7)····························

BE ALL THAT YOU CAN BE

Sharpay and Ryan can't believe Troy and Gabriella made the callbacks. After all, they didn't even try out. So the drama club co-captains devise a plan to keep Troy and Gabriella from singing at the callbacks. They convince Ms. Darbus to schedule the callbacks at the same time as the scholastic decathlon competition and the basketball championship game. This will eliminate Troy and Gabriella from the competition for the leads in the musical and keep Sharpay and Ryan on top. But Troy, Gabriella, and their friends think up a plan of their own. Timing's going to be crucial.

> **Gabi says:**
> Sharpay and Ryan are being tricky and cruel! Don't ever do this, because you could lose friends this way.

At just the right moment Taylor and Gabriella electronically shut down the lights and scoreboard in the gym from a remote laptop. Minutes later they use the same computer to cause a glitch with an experiment at the decathlon competition. Both buildings have to be evacuated quickly. Gabriella and Troy dash over to the East High theater...followed by everyone from the gym and the science room. It's crazy—but so far the plan is coming together perfectly! But now it appears that Troy and Gabriella arrive too late. Ms. Darbus reminds them that the theater waits for no one! And besides, they don't have an accompanist. But wait...Kelsi's still on stage and ready to go. Much to Sharpay's and Ryan's disgust, Troy and Gabriella get to sing. That's show biz!

Gabi says:
It's good for Gabriella and Troy that they made it to the callbacks in spite of what Sharpay and Ryan did. That's why it's important to never give up. You can go straight to the top if you really try hard.

Unbelievable! Troy and Gabriella rock the house singing "Breaking Free" and win the leads for the winter musical. They've broken free from the way others saw them that was different from who they really are. And they were able to do it with their friends dancing, clapping, and cheering them on. They've nailed the tune, and they're experiencing the fun and freedom of being themselves. The sky's the limit with this new freedom and confidence.

Do you ever feel like you want to run as fast as you possibly can until you crash through an invisible barrier that seems to be holding you back? Maybe for you it's a situation like Troy and Gabriella's where you don't feel like people know who you really are. Have you found yourself sitting on the edge of your bed at night wishing people could know the "real" you? Or maybe the problem is that you don't know who you really are because you've been allowing other people to mold and shape you.

> **Gabi says:**
> If you let others control your life, you will never be able to know the real you. That's why it's good to let God control your life.

HOW DOES THE WORLD SEE YOU?

As a teenager, I always did well in academics and sports, but my passion was music. It was my life and my identity. I was known as the "drummer dude." So when I went to my high-school class reunion, people thought I was still doing the music gig. They'd come up and say, "Hey, Russo. Who are you playing with now?" When I responded that I now work in full-time Christian ministry, they didn't know what to say. It was almost like I told them I had some strange tropical disease that was highly contagious! They'd politely say "bye" and quickly walk away. All through high school everybody had my identity wrapped up in the drums. And so did I.

Being confused over who you are can work the opposite way, too. For example, if you can't perform like others expect or you don't have the status or bling your friends say you need, you start thinking you're worthless. You may see yourself as a "loser" because you didn't make good grades in a certain class or because you got cut from the basketball team. Or maybe you've heard for a long time from your parents, teachers, and even friends that you'll never succeed in anything.

Gabi says:
If you let others control your life through high school, you and your parents and your friends will never know who you really are. Say people force you into playing soccer, but your real passion is art. People will be confused about who you really are.

I took a speech/communications class my freshman year of college. One day the professor asked me to stay after class.

"Mr. Russo, there's one thing I want to encourage you never to consider for a career—public speaking," she said. "You mumble. You don't look good when you're in front of people. You just don't have what it takes." It's a good thing I didn't follow her advice. Today I speak to audiences all over the world, face-to-face in events and at schools, on radio, and on TV! I'd like to find that professor today and see what she has to say. I broke free and so can you.

The world according to East High saw Troy as the basketball boy and Gabriella as the freaky math girl. But that didn't stop them from reaching for a place where they could be all that they could be. Don't let

> **Gabi says:**
> Just like in "Breaking Free," you need to break out of your shell and show people your real identity.

anyone keep you from discovering who you really are—and living it.

Faith in God can give you the strength to believe in yourself and discover your identity. It builds in your life until it becomes just like a wave the ocean can't control, then you break free and begin to live like the "real person" you were meant to be. You'll feel like there's no limit to what you can achieve!

DISCOVERING THE REAL YOU

Who are you? Not who do others think you are, but who is the real you? Who you are is determined by much more than what you have, what you do, or what you achieve. Telling me your name, where you live, where you go to school, or what you like to do are things about you. But you still haven't told me who you really are.

When you discover the real you, the way you think about life radically changes. Uncovering your identity makes you feel secure, important, and accepted. Then you can be the same person wherever you are—at home, at school, in your neighborhood—and whatever you're doing. But lots of people don't know how to find their identity, and even when they do, sometimes they don't want to believe it. They're afraid they might have to be someone they don't want to be.

Gabi says:
Martin Luther King Jr. knew his true identity, and he didn't let anyone hold him back. He took a stand for everybody who was mistreated and showed the world that everyone should be free.

You become complete as a person and have meaning in your life when you realize that your true identity is found through a relationship with God. This happens when you decide to live your life for Jesus and like Jesus.

It's only in Jesus that we can find out who we really are. Jesus knows us better than anyone else—even better than we know ourselves—because He made us. He's the one who put us together, piece by piece, molecule by molecule. Check this out:

> You made all the delicate, inner parts of my body and knit me together in my mother's womb. Thank you for making me so wonderfully complex! Your workmanship is marvelous—how well I know it. Psalm 139:13–14

This is huge! Think about what these verses are saying. You and I are unique creations of God. We are not accidents or mistakes.

> For we are God's masterpiece. He has created us anew in Christ Jesus, so we can do the good things he planned for us long ago. Ephesians 2:10

Since God considers us His masterpieces, we shouldn't treat ourselves or others with disrespect.

Billions of people have been born and walked the face of this planet, yet there have never been any two who are exactly alike—not even identical twins. There is no one who has your combination of gifts, talents, and abilities. Just think how special we are to God and how much He loves us!

So don't get caught in the trap of letting someone else mold and shape you into living like someone you're not. Whether it's one person or a whole group of people, you can't be reaching for the stars if they're holding you back. Don't allow anyone else to define who you are except Jesus. He understands the pressures and temptations you face. He also has the power and ability to help you take a stand, and He makes it possible for you to become all that you were designed to be.

> **Gabi says:**
> Like Troy and Gabriella, even though your friends might think something different, you should always follow your dreams.

That's why knowing the real you changes the way you live and act. A lot of kids do dumb things and treat others badly because they don't know who they are. One of the big reasons some kids have problems with drugs, alcohol, eating disorders, and even premarital sex is because they don't feel secure, accepted, or important. Helping them find their true identity in Jesus could change all this by influencing and changing the way they live.

With Jesus we have everything we'll ever need to be all that we can be and to reach for the stars. We'll still want to have friends, do fun things, and eventually have a cool job, but everything is meaningless without knowing Jesus.

So how do you find the real you?

BREAK FREE

In "Breaking Free" Troy and Gabriella sing it's "more than hope, more than faith—this is truth." Ultimately, it is truth that will set you free. You can break free when you decide to live your life for Jesus and like Jesus. Check out what He said about truth and being free:

> And you will know the truth, and the truth will set you free. John 8:32

Jesus not only tells the truth; He is the truth.

The truth is that God has a plan for your life. Listen to this promise found in Jeremiah 29:11:

> "For I know the plans I have for you," says the Lord. "They are plans for good and not for disaster, to give you a future and a hope."

Gabi says:
Jesus can lead you to be the best you can be in your life. Be sure to follow Him.

God wants you to get the most out of life. When you have secured your eternal destiny and identity through Christ, it should affect the quality of life you live here on earth. There will always be problems, pressures, and struggles, but the way you respond is going to be much different. Now you have all the resources of the living God giving you power to enable you to face the tough times in life. Only a loving God would make all this possible for us. The Bible says our minds can't even begin to imagine what God has planned for us to experience (see 1 Corinthians 2:9).

So why aren't more people experiencing this kind of life?

Because there's another part to the truth about us that Jesus is talking about. It's about a spiritual terminal disease that we're all born with, and it's called sin. "For everyone has sinned; we all fall short of God's glorious standard" (Romans 3:23). And there are consequences for our sin. "For the wages of sin is death, but the free gift of God is eternal life through Christ Jesus our Lord" (Romans 6:23).

> **Gabi says:**
> Adam and Eve sinned and were punished for what they did in disobeying God. And everyone has sinned just like them. That's why we need Jesus.

Sin is not being able to measure up to God's holy standard. Sin is also wrong thoughts, words, and actions. There are some sins that seem bigger than others, like murder or stealing. But all sins separate us from God. Sin is also an attitude that says, "I can live my life without God—I don't need Him." Look at the way *sin* is spelled. What's right in the middle? "I." Ultimately, the very heart of sin is trying to live your life without God. Everyone is born with this attitude and needs Jesus.

God is holy, without sin—and because of our sin, He cannot have a relationship with us. But the good news is that all sin can be forgiven and we can

Gabi says:
Just look back at the word **sin**. Most of your bad thoughts and actions roll around that middle letter "I." Sin is really being selfish, like when you lie, cheat, steal, or say bad things about other people. Don't let sin control your life.

receive His free gift of eternal life—living in heaven with Him after we die. God loves us so much that He made this possible. "But God showed his great love for us by sending Christ to die for us while we were still sinners" (Romans 5:8). This is amazing! Think about it! God sent His only son, Jesus, to die for us (take the punishment for our sin), not because we were good enough, but because He loved us. And it gets even better. Jesus not only died on a cross for our sin, but He rose from the grave after three days—that's why we celebrate at Easter. He's alive right now and wants to live inside you.

If you ever doubt God's love, remember that He showed you how much He loves you even before you knew about Him. Eternal life is not something we can earn, and it doesn't need to be paid back, because it's a gift. This precious gift not only guarantees us a place in heaven after we die, but it also gives us the power we need for this life.

You can't know the real you without Jesus. He is the only one who can truly set you free to be all that you were created to be. "So if the Son sets you free, you are truly free" (John 8:36). People struggle with their identity because they have not made the choice to receive God's free gift. God is a gentleman and will not force himself on anyone. He will not make anybody love Him. It's a decision you must make for yourself.

Gabi says:
Everyone should experience God's forgiveness, because you can celebrate His love for you.

WHAT ABOUT YOU?

Have you decided to live your life for Jesus and like Jesus yet? Have you received God's free gift of eternal life? If it's hard for you to understand this, you're not alone. But there's more—like trying to understand how God punished Jesus for your sin, what it means to be forgiven, having a new power for living, discovering your true identity, and having a place in heaven when you die. It's all a result of God's supernatural work. Don't panic or get frustrated. Remember, we're talking about some awesome supernatural stuff; God doesn't expect us to grasp everything all at once. He only expects us to take the first step, and then He will guide us in our spiritual journey.

Have you ever thought about all the different stuff we use every day and how it works? If you stop and think about some of these things, it can make your brain hurt! I've never been able to understand how electricity works or how water gets into the pipes and comes out in the shower, yet we still use electricity every day and take showers at least every other day (I hope!).

And I still don't understand how my cell phone works. How does it connect with other phones, and what do all the terms like SID, ESN, PCS, GSM, CDMA, and TDMA really mean? I read an article once that said they're really just very sophisticated radios. But if you ever see the inside of one, you'd realize they're probably one of the most complex things we use every day. Even though we don't understand what makes a cell phone work, that doesn't stop us from using it. Millions of people around the world use them constantly.

When you decide to live your life for Jesus and like Jesus, you may not totally understand everything that's involved in having a relationship with God. But the more you read the Bible, the more you pray, and the more you allow God to teach you, the more you will learn and understand. You grow in your relationship with God one day at a time. The hardest part is deciding to take that first step of commitment.

But keep in mind this decision will be costly. It will cost you your favorite sins and your self-centered attitude to try to live your life without God. It may cost you some friends who don't understand why your life is so different. The decision to follow Jesus may even cost you your current dreams about the future—because God may have something planned for you that is totally different from what you ever expected and much better than you could have ever imagined. That's what happened to me. The cost to accept Christ is high, but it's not anywhere near what it will cost you to reject Him.

If you're ready to start living your life for Jesus and like Jesus, take a few minutes right now and follow the steps listed below. It's a simple way to establish a relationship with the living God. Deciding to live your life for Jesus and like Jesus is the most important decision you will ever make. There's nothing greater than experiencing God's love, forgiveness, and acceptance. Once you've made this decision, your life is going to start changing.

It's not complicated, and you can do it right now. Check out this promise from the Bible:

> If you confess with your mouth that Jesus is Lord and believe in your heart that God raised him from the dead, you will be saved. Romans 10:9

Here's how you can begin your relationship with Jesus—become a Christian:

1. Admit that you are a sinner.
2. Be willing to turn away from your sins (repent).
3. Believe that Jesus Christ died for you on the cross and rose from the grave.
4. Through prayer, surrender your life to Jesus and ask Him to be in charge of your life through the Holy Spirit.

Pray something like this:

Dear Jesus,

I know that I have sinned and need your forgiveness. I want to turn away from my sins to live my life for you and like you. I believe that you died on the cross to take the penalty for my sins and that you came back to life after three days. I surrender my heart and life to you. I want you to save me from the punishment of my sins, and I want to follow you as the boss of my life. Thank you for your love and your gift of eternal life.

In Jesus' name, amen.

Did you decide to live your life for Jesus and like Jesus? If so, you've made the most important decision of your life! If you have sincerely accepted Jesus, then you can trust Him. Check out what the Bible says in Romans 10:13:

Everyone who calls on the name of the Lord will be saved.

When we surrender our lives to Jesus, we become brand-new people. Check out the promise in 2 Corinthians 5:17:

This means that anyone who belongs to Christ has become a new person. The old life is gone; a new life has begun!

Gabi says:
Whenever anyone accepts Christ, the angels in heaven celebrate and throw a big party. They are excited because there's a new member in God's family.

We may still look the same on the outside, but God makes us totally new people on the inside—we're not the same person anymore. You don't just change some stuff in your life; you start a new one—this time with a new

116

Master. God supernaturally changes us the minute we accept Jesus. We now have a close relationship with Him because sin no longer separates us. That's why it's important now to take time each day to grow even closer in our relationship with God. We can do this by studying the Bible and talking with Him in prayer. Another thing that can really help us is to be involved with other Christians at church and in a youth group.

A new life in Jesus gives you a brand-new identity. Becoming a Christian is not just something you add to your life—it's something that becomes your life. You've been given an awesome new power to help you with the tough stuff in life. The power you now have is the same power that brought Jesus back to life from the grave on the very first Easter Sunday. It's called resurrection power, and it can help with all the difficult issues and pain in your life. This power never runs out, and you can only get it from the living God of the Bible.

This is something no other religion can offer. But there's a catch. In order to get this new life, you have to surrender the old one. You must give up control and decide to live your life for Jesus, not for yourself.

When it comes to Jesus and the kingdom of God, things are just the opposite. Jesus told his followers this:

> If you try to hang on to your life, you will lose it. But if you give up your life for my sake, you will save it. Matthew 16:25

Surrendering to someone else is always hard, because you no longer maintain control. But you are not surrendering to just anyone—you're surrendering to the Creator God, the one who made you and knows what is best for you. The only way we can experience real purpose in our lives, as well as wisdom for the tough stuff we face, is by surrendering our lives to Jesus.

This relationship that you have established is one that cannot be broken or ended. Jesus promises to never let you down and never give you up (see Hebrews 13:5). This is the heart of Christianity. It's not a religion; it's God revealing himself to us, rescuing us from our sin, and making it possible for us to experience a relationship with Him.

You may feel totally different now or you may not. The most important thing is that you have started this relationship with the living God, and you have the rest of eternity to develop and experience it!

KEEPING YOUR HEAD AND YOUR HEART IN THE GAME (OF LIFE)

Do people at school know who you really are? Maybe, like Troy and Gabriella, you've got a talent that no one else knows about. This week tell someone about it. Think about who is the right person to share it with. And ask that person if they like to do something that others don't know about. Don't forget to pray and ask God to help you do this.

Also, think about friends you have who may not have a relationship with God. Ask God to help you tell others what has happened in your life and why you decided to live it for Jesus and like Jesus. Invite them to an activity at your church or to a Christian event in the area. Pray for your friends every day.

If you recently decided to live your life for Jesus and like Jesus, here are some things to remember: As you would do in any other relationship, don't forget to stay in touch with Jesus, your new best friend. You can do this in a couple of ways. Start by reading the letters Jesus has already given you that tell about who He is, how He can help you, how to live your life, and how much He loves you. All this and much more is found in the Bible. Take time each day to read and study a portion of it. One good place to start is in the Old Testament book called Proverbs. There's one chapter for each day of the month, and it's packed with practical advice about life stuff. And just like you might instant-message a friend on the Internet, you can also send an instant message to God through prayer. You can pray anytime and anyplace, and you don't even have to be online!

Life isn't always easy today. Broken families, money problems, unrealistic expectations from friends and parents, abuse, and stress can get you down. Don't get too overwhelmed. Learn to trust God. Take it one day at a time. When you learn to rely on Him with the small things, it will be easier to deal with the big stuff when it happens.

Make sure you get plugged in to a church where they teach from the Bible about Jesus, and where you can worship and develop friendships with other Christians. Remember to tell others what Jesus has done for you, because they can experience the same thing. And look for ways to serve God by helping others in need in the world.

By the way, if you decided to start living your life for Jesus and like Jesus, please let me know by using the contact information in the back of this book. This is just the beginning of a great new life with Jesus. I want to pray for you and send you some stuff—including a CD—to help you get started growing in this new relationship with God.

8

MAKING EACH OTHER STRONG

WOW! What a day! Troy and Gabriella rock the house with their singing. The lights and scoreboard are working again, so Chad, Troy, and the rest of the Wildcats sprint back to the gym while Taylor, Gabriella, and the rest of the decathlon team hurry back to the competition. In the final seconds of the big game, Troy nails a basket and the championship belongs to East High. Coach Bolton couldn't be happier!

The air in the gym is electric and the celebration is only just beginning. Taylor, Gabriella, and the rest of the decathlon team have also won the scholastic competition. Gabriella's telling Troy the good news when she gets interrupted by Taylor, who's totally excited because Chad has just asked her to go with him to the big after-party. Sharpay congratulates Gabriella and tells her to "break a leg"—"good luck" in showbiz talk. Troy makes the "playmaker" Kelsi's day by giving her the game ball.

There's a whistle in the background; the Wildcats' drum line kicks it with a cadence, and the gym erupts as people start dancing and singing. Things are different at East High now—and it looks like they'll stay that way. It's been an interesting adventure since everyone returned from Christmas vacation. People have changed. Troy, Gabriella, Chad, Taylor—even Ryan and Sharpay—all want to be there for each other. Everybody has realized that people should be able to do what they're passionate about and not stay limited by the stereotypes others have placed on them. It's all about appreciating others for who they are and what they do. Together, they're gonna be there for each other every time.

> **Gabi says:**
> It's good for everyone to follow their dreams! God has special dreams for you, and He has great things He wants you to accomplish. You can't imagine all that God has planned for you. It's amazing!

Jocks, brainiacs, members of the drama club, and others have all realized that everyone is special and different in their own way—and that's a good thing! These differences no longer divide the school; they've actually brought everybody together.

It's time to celebrate and say no to the status quo. Together is where they belong. Together they can make their dreams come true. Sounds like the Wildcats will never be the same again!

WE NEED EACH OTHER

Troy, Gabriella, Taylor, Chad, Sharpay, Ryan, and the rest of the East High Wildcats learned a valuable lesson—we really do need each other. No one likes to feel isolated and alone. There's security, encouragement, and strength when we're with others. Remember the wise guy named Solomon? He came to this same conclusion and wrote about it centuries ago in the Bible.

> Two people are better off than one, for they can help each other succeed. If one person falls, the other can reach out and help. But someone who falls alone is in real trouble. Likewise, two people lying close together can keep each other warm. But how can one be warm alone? A person standing alone can be attacked and defeated, but two can stand back-to-back and conquer. Three are even better, for a triple-braided cord is not easily broken. Ecclesiastes 4:9–12

Even though Solomon wrote these words a long, long time ago, they're still true for us today. Life is designed for friendship, not isolation; for closeness, not loneliness. Some people try to go it alone because they don't think they can trust others. But you can't live like this for very long. Someday you'll have to learn to trust someone. We're all in this life together, and we need each other. We're not here on this planet to serve ourselves, but to serve God and others. Don't isolate yourself and try to go it alone. Seek friends and be a team member. There's no limitation to what we can accomplish working together.

> **Gabi says:**
> Friendship is the most important thing that can happen. In everyday life you need God and good friends. It's a great mix!

Chances are the school you go to is more like the way East High used to be. But just imagine how different things would be if the people on your campus and at schools across the country felt the same way Troy, Gabriella, Sharpay, Ryan, and the rest of the kids did at East High. There wouldn't be any cliques and people wouldn't worry about getting bullied. Imagine what it would be like if everybody got along—no matter what the color of their skin or what music they listened to or how they dressed. Think about how different things would be without the threat of violence or drug and alcohol abuse. There'd be no need to have speakers like me come to a campus for an assembly during Red Ribbon Week. Wouldn't it be great if students started speaking with one voice and supported each other as they pursued their dreams?

Gabi says:
Wouldn't it be great if the whole world stopped racism and violence? Then we would have peace with one another.

THE PROBLEM OF ME

Part of the reason this isn't happening is because we live in a highly competitive and comparative world. We're bombarded with messages in the media every day telling us how we should dress or style our hair, what food to eat and drink—even the right toothpaste to use! The list is endless. We end up comparing ourselves with others and against the false standards of our society. Somehow we've started believing that someone who doesn't meet these crazy standards is a loser and doesn't really matter. It's become the attitude to have even though no one ever really says, "You need to think, feel, and live this way." Society teaches us to put others down rather than treat them special because they're different than we are. It's this kind of thinking that keeps us from working together.

Things get even more complicated because of the "it's all about me" attitude. This 'tude seems to be pretty popular as more and more people think the thing to do is to become "me-centered." We don't care about other people and are only worried about ourselves. Consequently, we've lost respect for ourselves and for others. It's time to start realizing that it's not about *me*—it's about *we*. Turn your eyes around and stop looking at yourself. Take a look at others around you. Become more aware of their needs, hopes, and ideas. Together is where we belong. Think about how many dreams could come true if we'd adopt this 'tude.

> **Gabi says:**
> If we stopped thinking about ourselves and started thinking about others more, many of the problems in the world would not even exist.

CHANGING OUR 'TUDE

The only way the 'tude is going to change is if it starts in the heart. We need some supernatural help.

Earlier in the book we talked about each of us being unique creations of God. If we're going to learn to be there for each other every time, we need to understand just how special every person really is in God's eyes.

Let's go way back to the beginning of the Owner's Manual—the Bible.

> So God created human beings in his own image. In the image of God he created them; male and female he created them. Genesis 1:27

Unbelievable! Each and every person is created equal in God's image. It doesn't say only certain individuals or groups—it says everyone. The Bible doesn't make a distinction between males and females or even the color of your skin. It says *everyone* is made in God's image. Putting yourself or others down is criticizing what God has made. When you're jealous and want what someone else has, you're really saying that God made a mistake. He wants us to learn to celebrate our differences.

Gabi says:
The "treasure map"—the Bible—can show us all the ways we need to live life. That's why it's important to study it every day.

Since God has no physical body, we can't be exactly like Him, so what does it mean to be created in His image? Part of being created in His image is the ability we have to reflect

His character in our kindness, patience, forgiveness, and love toward one another.

That's how special we are. And knowing this should influence the way we treat others—and ourselves. It's hard to treat someone else with respect if you don't respect yourself. Remember, you can still respect someone even if you don't like them or agree with everything they do and say.

> **Gabi says:**
> If you respect yourself, you'll be nicer to everyone and be a lot happier.

Just think about how different your world would be if you looked at others with a special set of lenses that allowed you to see them as being created in the image of God. Now you'd be looking at the heart rather than the outside—you'd see the real person.

Imagine how much more we could accomplish by standing together hand in hand. There's a lot of stuff in our world that needs to be changed, and together there's no limit on how much we can do to make a difference. Instead of putting up walls between us, let's tear them down.

We're all in this life together; we need each other. When we all come together, we make each other strong. And when we're strong, we can make all our dreams come true, and our world becomes a better place to live.

KEEPING YOUR HEAD AND YOUR HEART IN THE GAME (OF LIFE)

Sometimes it's hard to like someone else and appreciate them for who they are and for their talents because we don't like ourselves. Is this true for you? Because we are made in God's image, we can feel positive about ourselves. Knowing that God loves you and that you're valuable to Him can give you the ability to help others around you.

Take some time each day to thank God for the way He has made you. Make a list of all the things that are unique about you, including talents, abilities, and physical characteristics. Learn to appreciate all the things God has blessed you with as you use them to serve Him and others.

What kinds of things would you like to see changed at your school? Are there others you know who feel the same way? Get with others and start praying about how God could use you together to change your school—and the world!

THE LOOK

Okay, how many times have you watched the *High School Musical* DVD? You've probably seen it more than once. And if you're like Gabi, you've listened to the CD so much that you know every lyric to every song perfectly! Should I admit now that I actually have the soundtrack on my iPod . . . and that sometimes I even listen to it when Gabi's not with me? . . . Nah . . . I don't need any more embarrassing moments!

Gabi says:
LOL

Isn't it cool how they have all the bonus features on the DVDs? Did you watch the music video of "I Can't Take My Eyes Off of You"? It's a great tune. And it's even better live, in person!

For Gabi's birthday I took her and her older sister, Kati, to see the High School Musical Live concert when the tour came to

Gabi says:
I could hardly wait for that night to come when I found out Dad got tickets for the concert!

Southern California. Gabi's older brother, Tony, didn't come because he had to work that night. We had unbelievable seats—four rows from the stage on the left side. Does it get any better?!

After arriving early to the concert and grabbing something

Gabi says:
Lucas is so funny! And the concert was awesome! It was fun making new friends and taking some pictures together. I really liked sitting so close to the stage because I felt like I could almost reach out and touch the cast. It was a great experience to see them in person and hear all the songs live. And it was cool to see Corbin jump up on the stage with the fireworks. I really liked the way Ashley and Lucas sang "Bop to the Top."

to eat, we found our seats. Right away Gabi was able to make some new friends of the people sitting behind us. Just before the concert started, they all took pictures together and exchanged e-mail addresses. Memories!

The show was awesome! The sound . . . the lights . . . the huge screen media . . . the special effects . . . the live band . . . It was an experience we will not soon forget! Plus, all the main characters from the movie, except Zach, were on stage to perform. I guess he was busy filming another movie. Lucas did a great job as the host for the concert.

Then, mixed in with all our favorite songs from the movie, we also got to hear mini concerts from Corbin, Ashley, and Vanessa featuring tunes from their new solo CD releases. Good stuff!

CAN'T TAKE HIS EYES OFF OF YOU

Besides being a catchy dance tune musically, "I Can't Take My Eyes Off of You" has some interesting things to think about lyrically. The song took on new meaning for me after seeing it performed live in concert. The words of the song sum up a main theme of this book—keeping your head and your heart in the game (of life). And what it all comes down to is where your eyes are and who has your heart.

But first, have you ever wondered where God's eyes are? They're on you! That probably never even crossed your mind before. And there's something else you may not know: He never takes His eyes off of you! Why? It's because of His awesome love and care for you. Job 36:7 says that God never takes His eyes off the innocent. His eyes also search the earth to strengthen us if our hearts are fully committed to Him (see

2 Chronicles 16:9). It's unbelievable to think that the God of the universe can't take His eyes off of us!

This should be a huge encouragement to you. It should also help you realize how significant you are in God's eyes. Just think, no matter where you are or what you're doing, God is always watching out for you. He is there to guide and help you in every situation. This will take some getting used to, but once you do, you'll start noticing some changes in your life.

> **Gabi says:**
> It's totally awesome that God is always watching out for us!

WHERE ARE YOUR EYES?

We live in a world filled with lots of eye candy. It's everywhere—on large plasma TV screens, small cell-phone screens, billboards, Internet sites, the beauty of nature—and that's just a small part of the list! Some of the eye candy is positive, while other stuff can be disgusting. That's why it's important to guard your eyes because it can affect your whole life. The Bible talks about this "spiritual vision" in Matthew 6:22–23:

> Your eye is a lamp that provides light for your body. When your eye is good, your whole body is filled with

light. But when your eye is bad, your whole body is filled with darkness.

God wants our spiritual vision to be sharp and clear so we can see the world from His point of view. But this spiritual insight can easily be clouded and distorted with the world's eye candy. That's why it's important to keep our eyes focused on God. He's even given us a special set of glasses—a filter—to look at life through. It's the Bible. Make it a priority to look into it often and apply the things you are learning to your everyday life. Good eyes are focused on God. You can see everything you need right in His eyes.

Gabi says:
That is true! When you look into His eyes you can see help, trust, protection, strength, understanding, and love. Don't let other stuff distract you from keeping your eyes on God. You should always put your faith in Him.

The Bible describes life like a race in Hebrews 12:1-2:

> Therefore, since we are surrounded by such a huge crowd of witnesses to the life of faith, let us strip off every weight that slows us down, especially the sin that so easily trips us up. And let us run with endurance the that God has set before us. We do this by keeping our

eyes on Jesus, the champion who initiates and perfects our faith. Because of the joy awaiting Him, he endured the cross, disregarding its shame. Now he is seated in the place of honor beside God's throne.

We need to remember that life isn't a sprint—it's a long-distance race. And to run this race God has planned for us will require lots of discipline and staying power. We can do this by keeping our eyes on Jesus, who is our example and gives us the courage we need to finish this race well.

WHO'S GOT YOUR HEART?

Just like there is a lot of eye candy in the world, there are also a lot of things that can cause heart pollution. Our hearts are like incredible digital recording devices that constantly record and store what we see, hear, and study. That's why it's so important to carefully filter everything that goes into it. You may be thinking, *What? I thought my heart pumped blood around my body.* It does. But when we read the word *heart* in the Bible, it symbolizes what makes us a person deep inside. It's our feelings of love and desire. Do you see now why we need to protect it?

Heart pollution is serious stuff. Look at what Proverbs 4:23 says:

Guard your heart above all else, for it determines the course of your life.

So how do you guard your heart? By using God's Word as a filter and being careful what you put in your heart. What kinds of music do you listen to? Which DVDs and TV shows do you watch? What sites do you visit online? How about the books you read? All of this and more can end up stored in your heart. You might need God's help in cleaning out your heart because of what's been recorded and stored. Don't allow your heart to become polluted.

> **Gabi says:**
> Make sure God is always number one in your heart.

It's important to concentrate on the desires that will keep us on the right path in life. We have to be careful that we don't go after everything we see. We may end up getting sidetracked into sin. From now on let God have your heart.

ONE FINAL THOUGHT

The key to keeping your head and your heart in the game is to keep your eyes on Jesus. Just like God can't take His eyes off you, I hope you feel the same way, too!

> **Gabi says:**
> A good rhyme to remember!

CONTACT INFORMATION

For more information on other resources, radio and TV shows, *Real Answers* evangelistic events, and "Choices" school assemblies, please contact:

Real Answers With Steve Russo

P.O. Box 1549

Ontario, California 91762

909-466-7060

909-466-7056 FAX

Russoteam@realanswers.com

www.realanswers.com